Poetry Out Loud:
National Recitation Contest

NATIONAL ENDOWMENT FOR THE ARTS
and
THE POETRY FOUNDATION
present

THE ANTHOLOGY

Poems for

Poetry Out Loud:
National Recitation Contest

Edited by
DAN STONE
and
STEPHEN YOUNG

DESIGN BY WINTERHOUSE STUDIO
WINTERHOUSE.COM

The National Endowment for the Arts is the largest annual funder of the arts in the United States. An independent federal agency, the NEA is the official arts organization of the United States government, dedicated to supporting excellence in the arts — both new and established — bringing the arts to all Americans, and providing leadership in arts education.

The Poetry Foundation is an independent literary organization committed to a vigorous presence for poetry in our culture. The Foundation publishes *Poetry* magazine, sponsors a variety of public programs, and supports creative projects in literature.

The ear is the only true writer and the only true reader.
—*Robert Frost*

INTRODUCTION

The *Poetry Out Loud Anthology* presents only a fraction of the poems available to participants. The full selection, which will be expanded regularly, can be found online at www.poetryoutloud.org. There, students and teachers will find a great variety of classic and contemporary poetry that couldn't be included here because of space and copyright restrictions.

A great poem may be preserved on the page, but it lives when it is spoken and heard. For many students, performance can be a much more exciting entry into literature than a simple reading assignment. Consider the popularity of the slam and spoken word movement — events that create dynamic communities of speakers and listeners. Students who learn poems by heart own them for life. And they can always be shared, whether the audience is oneself or the world at large.

The National Endowment for the Arts and the Poetry Foundation are proud to present *Poetry Out Loud* to high school students across the nation.

DAN STONE
National Endowment for the Arts

STEPHEN YOUNG
Poetry Foundation

CONTENTS

POEMS

NOTES & CREDITS

POEMS

MATTHEW ARNOLD

Dover Beach

The sea is calm tonight.
The tide is full, the moon lies fair
Upon the straits; on the French coast the light
Gleams and is gone; the cliffs of England stand,
Glimmering and vast, out in the tranquil bay.
Come to the window, sweet is the night-air!
Only, from the long line of spray
Where the sea meets the moon-blanched land,
Listen! you hear the grating roar
Of pebbles which the waves draw back, and fling,
At their return, up the high strand,
Begin, and cease, and then again begin,
With tremulous cadence slow, and bring
The eternal note of sadness in.

Sophocles long ago
Heard it on the Ægean, and it brought
Into his mind the turbid ebb and flow
Of human misery; we
Find also in the sound a thought,
Hearing it by this distant northern sea.

The Sea of Faith
Was once, too, at the full, and round earth's shore
Lay like the folds of a bright girdle furled.
But now I only hear
Its melancholy, long, withdrawing roar,
Retreating, to the breath
Of the night-wind, down the vast edges drear
And naked shingles of the world.

Ah, love, let us be true
To one another! for the world, which seems
To lie before us like a land of dreams,
So various, so beautiful, so new,
Hath really neither joy, nor love, nor light,
Nor certitude, nor peace, nor help for pain;
And we are here as on a darkling plain
Swept with confused alarms of struggle and flight,
Where ignorant armies clash by night.

W.H. AUDEN

The Unknown Citizen

(To JS/07/M/378
This Marble Monument
Is Erected by the State)

He was found by the Bureau of Statistics to be
One against whom there was no official complaint,
And all the reports on his conduct agree
That, in the modern sense of an old-fashioned word, he was a saint,
For in everything he did he served the Greater Community.
Except for the War till the day he retired
He worked in a factory and never got fired,
But satisfied his employers, Fudge Motors Inc.
Yet he wasn't a scab or odd in his views,
For his Union reports that he paid his dues,
(Our report on his Union shows it was sound)
And our Social Psychology workers found
That he was popular with his mates and liked a drink.
The Press are convinced that he bought a paper every day
And that his reactions to advertisements were normal in every way.
Policies taken out in his name prove that he was fully insured,
And his Health-card shows he was once in a hospital but left it cured.
Both Producers Research and High-Grade Living declare
He was fully sensible to the advantages of the Installment Plan
And had everything necessary to the Modern Man,
A phonograph, a radio, a car and a frigidaire.
Our researchers into Public Opinion are content
That he held the proper opinions for the time of year;
When there was peace, he was for peace; when there was war, he went.
He was married and added five children to the population,
Which our Eugenist says was the right number for a parent of his
    generation,
And our teachers report that he never interfered with their education.
Was he free? Was he happy? The question is absurd:
Had anything been wrong, we should certainly have heard.

The More Loving One

Looking up at the stars, I know quite well
That, for all they care, I can go to hell,
But on earth indifference is the least
We have to dread from man or beast.

How should we like it were stars to burn
With a passion for us we could not return?
If equal affection cannot be,
Let the more loving one be me.

Admirer as I think I am
Of stars that do not give a damn,
I cannot, now I see them, say
I missed one terribly all day.

Were all stars to disappear or die,
I should learn to look at an empty sky
And feel its total dark sublime,
Though this might take me a little time.

Love Armed

Song from Abdelazar

Love in Fantastic Triumph sat,
Whilst Bleeding Hearts around him flowed,
For whom Fresh pains he did Create,
And strange Tyrannic power he showed;
From thy Bright Eyes he took his fire,
Which round about, in sport he hurled;
But 'twas from mine he took desire
Enough to undo the Amorous World.

From me he took his sighs and tears,
From thee his Pride and Cruelty;
From me his Languishments and Fears,
And every Killing Dart from thee;
Thus thou and I, the God have armed,
And set him up a Deity;
But my poor Heart alone is harmed,
Whilst thine the Victor is, and free.

AMBROSE BIERCE

The New Decalogue

Have but one God: thy knees were sore
If bent in prayer to three or four.

Adore no images save those
The coinage of thy country shows.

Take not the Name in vain. Direct
Thy swearing unto some effect.

Thy hand from Sunday work be held—
Work not at all unless compelled.

Honor thy parents, and perchance
Their wills thy fortunes may advance.

Kill not—death liberates thy foe
From persecution's constant woe.

Kiss not thy neighbor's wife. Of course
There's no objection to divorce.

To steal were folly, for 'tis plain
In cheating there is greater gain.

Bear not false witness. Shake your head
And say that you have "heard it said."

Who stays to covet ne'er will catch
An opportunity to snatch.

WILLIAM BLAKE

The Tyger

Tyger! Tyger! burning bright
In the forests of the night,
What immortal hand or eye
Could frame thy fearful symmetry?

In what distant deeps or skies
Burnt the fire of thine eyes?
On what wings dare he aspire?
What the hand dare seize the fire?

And what shoulder, and what art,
Could twist the sinews of thy heart?
And when thy heart began to beat,
What dread hand? and what dread feet?

What the hammer? what the chain?
In what furnace was thy brain?
What the anvil? what dread grasp
Dare its deadly terrors clasp?

When the stars threw down their spears,
And watered heaven with their tears,
Did he smile his work to see?
Did he who made the Lamb make thee?

Tyger! Tyger! burning bright
In the forests of the night,
What immortal hand or eye,
Dare frame thy fearful symmetry?

LOUISE BOGAN

Women

Women have no wilderness in them,
They are provident instead,
Content in the tight hot cell of their hearts
To eat dusty bread.

They do not see cattle cropping red winter grass,
They do not hear
Snow water going down under culverts
Shallow and clear.

They wait, when they should turn to journeys,
They stiffen, when they should bend.
They use against themselves that benevolence
To which no man is friend.

They cannot think of so many crops to a field
Or of clean wood cleft by an axe.
Their love is an eager meaninglessness
Too tense, or too lax.

They hear in every whisper that speaks to them
A shout and a cry.
As like as not, when they take life over their door-sills
They should let it go by.

ANNE BRADSTREET

To My Dear and Loving Husband

If ever two were one, then surely we.
If ever man were loved by wife, then thee.
If ever wife was happy in a man,
Compare with me, ye women, if you can.
I prize thy love more than whole mines of gold,
Or all the riches that the East doth hold.
My love is such that rivers cannot quench,
Nor ought but love from thee give recompense.
Thy love is such I can no way repay;
The heavens reward thee manifold, I pray.
Then while we live, in love let's so persever,
That when we live no more, we may live ever.

EMILY BRONTË

Shall earth no more inspire thee

Shall earth no more inspire thee,
Thou lonely dreamer now?
Since passion may not fire thee
Shall Nature cease to bow?

Thy mind is ever moving
In regions dark to thee;
Recall its useless roving—
Come back and dwell with me.

I know my mountain breezes
Enchant and soothe thee still—
I know my sunshine pleases
Despite thy wayward will.

When day with evening blending
Sinks from the summer sky,
I've seen thy spirit bending
In fond idolatry.

I've watched thee every hour;
I know my mighty sway,
I know my magic power
To drive thy griefs away.

Few hearts to mortals given
On earth so wildly pine;
Yet none would ask a heaven
More like this earth than thine.

Then let my winds caress thee;
Thy comrade let me be—
Since nought beside can bless thee,
Return and dwell with me.

RUPERT BROOKE

The Soldier

If I should die, think only this of me:
    That there's some corner of a foreign field
That is forever England. There shall be
    In that rich earth a richer dust concealed;
A dust whom England bore, shaped, made aware,
    Gave, once, her flowers to love, her ways to roam,
A body of England's, breathing English air,
    Washed by the rivers, blest by suns of home.

And think, this heart, all evil shed away,
    A pulse in the eternal mind, no less
        Gives somewhere back the thoughts by England given;
Her sights and sounds; dreams happy as her day;
    And laughter, learnt of friends; and gentleness,
        In hearts at peace, under an English heaven.

GWENDOLYN BROOKS

Sadie and Maud

Maud went to college.
Sadie stayed at home.
Sadie scraped life
With a fine-tooth comb.

She didn't leave a tangle in.
Her comb found every strand.
Sadie was one of the livingest chits
In all the land.

Sadie bore two babies
Under her maiden name.
Maud and Ma and Papa
Nearly died of shame.

When Sadie said her last so-long
Her girls struck out from home.
(Sadie had left as heritage
Her fine-tooth comb.)

Maud, who went to college,
Is a thin brown mouse.
She is living all alone
In this old house.

ELIZABETH BARRETT BROWNING

How do I love thee? Let me count the ways

How do I love thee? Let me count the ways.
I love thee to the depth and breadth and height
My soul can reach, when feeling out of sight
For the ends of being and ideal grace.
I love thee to the level of every day's
Most quiet need, by sun and candle-light.
I love thee freely, as men strive for right;
I love thee purely, as they turn from praise.
I love thee with the passion put to use
In my old griefs, and with my childhood's faith.
I love thee with a love I seemed to lose
With my lost saints. I love thee with the breath,
Smiles, tears, of all my life; and, if God choose,
I shall but love thee better after death.

ROBERT BROWNING

My Last Duchess

FERRARA

That's my last Duchess painted on the wall,
Looking as if she were alive. I call
That piece a wonder, now; Frà Pandolf's hands
Worked busily a day, and there she stands.
Will't please you sit and look at her? I said
"Frà Pandolf" by design, for never read
Strangers like you that pictured countenance,
The depth and passion of its earnest glance,
But to myself they turned (since none puts by
The curtain I have drawn for you, but I)
And seemed as they would ask me, if they durst,
How such a glance came there; so, not the first
Are you to turn and ask thus. Sir, 'twas not
Her husband's presence only, called that spot
Of joy into the Duchess' cheek; perhaps
Frà Pandolf chanced to say, "Her mantle laps
Over my lady's wrist too much," or "Paint
Must never hope to reproduce the faint
Half-flush that dies along her throat." Such stuff
Was courtesy, she thought, and cause enough
For calling up that spot of joy. She had
A heart—how shall I say?— too soon made glad,
Too easily impressed; she liked whate'er
She looked on, and her looks went everywhere.
Sir, 'twas all one! My favour at her breast,
The dropping of the daylight in the West,
The bough of cherries some officious fool
Broke in the orchard for her, the white mule
She rode with round the terrace—all and each
Would draw from her alike the approving speech,
Or blush, at least. She thanked men—good! but thanked
Somehow—I know not how—as if she ranked
My gift of a nine-hundred-years-old name
With anybody's gift. Who'd stoop to blame

This sort of trifling? Even had you skill
In speech—which I have not—to make your will
Quite clear to such an one, and say, "Just this
Or that in you disgusts me; here you miss,
Or there exceed the mark"—and if she let
Herself be lessoned so, nor plainly set
Her wits to yours, forsooth, and made excuse—
E'en then would be some stooping; and I choose
Never to stoop. Oh, sir, she smiled, no doubt,
Whene'er I passed her; but who passed without
Much the same smile? This grew; I gave commands;
Then all smiles stopped together. There she stands
As if alive. Will't please you rise? We'll meet
The company below, then. I repeat,
The Count your master's known munificence
Is ample warrant that no just pretense
Of mine for dowry will be disallowed;
Though his fair daughter's self, as I avowed
At starting, is my object. Nay, we'll go
Together down, sir. Notice Neptune, though,
Taming a sea-horse, thought a rarity,
Which Claus of Innsbruck cast in bronze for me!

ROBERT BURNS

A Red, Red Rose

O my Luve is like a red, red rose
    That's newly sprung in June;
O my Luve is like the melody
    That's sweetly played in tune.

So fair art thou, my bonnie lass,
    So deep in luve am I;
And I will luve thee still, my dear,
    Till a' the seas gang dry.

Till a' the seas gang dry, my dear,
    And the rocks melt wi' the sun;
I will love thee still, my dear,
    While the sands o' life shall run.

And fare thee weel, my only luve!
    And fare thee weel awhile!
And I will come again, my luve,
    Though it were ten thousand mile.

GEORGE GORDON, LORD BYRON

She Walks in Beauty

She walks in beauty, like the night
   Of cloudless climes and starry skies;
And all that's best of dark and bright
   Meet in her aspect and her eyes;
Thus mellowed to that tender light
   Which heaven to gaudy day denies.

One shade the more, one ray the less,
   Had half impaired the nameless grace
Which waves in every raven tress,
   Or softly lightens o'er her face;
Where thoughts serenely sweet express,
   How pure, how dear their dwelling-place.

And on that cheek, and o'er that brow,
   So soft, so calm, yet eloquent,
The smiles that win, the tints that glow,
   But tell of days in goodness spent,
A mind at peace with all below,
   A heart whose love is innocent!

THOMAS CAMPION

Follow thy fair sun, unhappy shadow

Follow thy fair sun, unhappy shadow,
Though thou be black as night
And she made all of light,
Yet follow thy fair sun unhappy shadow.

Follow her whose light thy light depriveth,
Though here thou liv'st disgraced,
And she in heaven is placed,
Yet follow her whose light the world reviveth.

Follow those pure beams whose beauty burneth,
That so have scorched thee,
As thou still black must be,
Till Her kind beams thy black to brightness turneth.

Follow her while yet her glory shineth,
There comes a luckless night,
That will dim all her light,
And this the black unhappy shade divineth.

Follow still since so thy fates ordained,
The Sun must have his shade,
Till both at once do fade,
The Sun still proved, the shadow still disdained.

LEWIS CARROLL

Jabberwocky

'Twas brillig, and the slithy toves
    Did gyre and gimble in the wabe:
All mimsy were the borogoves,
    And the mome raths outgrabe.

"Beware the Jabberwock, my son!
    The jaws that bite, the claws that catch!
Beware the Jubjub bird, and shun
    The frumious Bandersnatch!"

He took his vorpal sword in hand;
    Long time the manxome foe he sought—
So rested he by the Tumtum tree
    And stood awhile in thought.

And, as in uffish thought he stood,
    The Jabberwock, with eyes of flame,
Came whiffling through the tulgey wood,
    And burbled as it came!

One, two! One, two! And through and through
    The vorpal blade went snicker-snack!
He left it dead, and with its head
    He went galumphing back.

"And hast thou slain the Jabberwock?
    Come to my arms, my beamish boy!
O frabjous day! Callooh! Callay!"
    He chortled in his joy.

'Twas brillig, and the slithy toves
    Did gyre and gimble in the wabe:
All mimsy were the borogoves,
    And the mome raths outgrabe.

LADY MARY CHUDLEIGH

To the Ladies

Wife and servant are the same,
But only differ in the name:
For when that fatal knot is tied,
Which nothing, nothing can divide:
When she the word *obey* has said,
And man by law supreme has made,
Then all that's kind is laid aside,
And nothing left but state and pride:
Fierce as an Eastern prince he grows,
And all his innate rigour shows:
Then but to look, to laugh, or speak,
Will the nuptial contract break.
Like mutes she signs alone must make,
And never any freedom take:
But still be governed by a nod,
And fear her husband as a God:
Him still must serve, him still obey,
And nothing act, and nothing say,
But what her haughty lord thinks fit,
Who with the power, has all the wit.
Then shun, oh! shun that wretched state,
And all the fawning flatt'rers hate:
Value your selves, and men despise,
You must be proud, if you'll be wise.

JOHN CLARE

I Am

I am—yet what I am none cares or knows;
My friends forsake me like a memory lost:
I am the self-consumer of my woes—
They rise and vanish in oblivious host,
Like shadows in love's frenzied stifled throes
And yet I am, and live—like vapours tossed

Into the nothingness of scorn and noise,
Into the living sea of waking dreams,
Where there is neither sense of life or joys,
But the vast shipwreck of my life's esteems;
Even the dearest that I loved the best
Are strange—nay, rather, stranger than the rest.

I long for scenes where man hath never trod
A place where woman never smiled or wept
There to abide with my Creator, God,
And sleep as I in childhood sweetly slept,
Untroubling and untroubled where I lie
The grass below—above the vaulted sky.

LUCILLE CLIFTON

[*if mama / could see*]

if mama
could see
she would see
lucy sprawling
limbs of lucy
decorating the
backs of chairs
lucy hair
holding the mirrors up
that reflect odd
aspects of lucy.

if mama
could hear
she would hear
lucysong rolled in the
corners like lint
exotic webs of lucysighs
long lucy spiders explaining
to obscure gods.

if mama
could talk
she would talk
good girl
good girl
good girl
clean up your room.

SAMUEL TAYLOR COLERIDGE

Kubla Khan

Or, a vision in a dream. A Fragment.

In Xanadu did Kubla Khan
A stately pleasure-dome decree:
Where Alph, the sacred river, ran
Through caverns measureless to man
    Down to a sunless sea.
So twice five miles of fertile ground
With walls and towers were girdled round;
And there were gardens bright with sinuous rills,
Where blossomed many an incense-bearing tree;
And here were forests ancient as the hills,
Enfolding sunny spots of greenery.

But oh! that deep romantic chasm which slanted
Down the green hill athwart a cedarn cover!
A savage place! as holy and enchanted
As e'er beneath a waning moon was haunted
By woman wailing for her demon-lover!
And from this chasm, with ceaseless turmoil seething,
As if this earth in fast thick pants were breathing,
A mighty fountain momently was forced:
Amid whose swift half-intermitted burst
Huge fragments vaulted like rebounding hail,
Or chaffy grain beneath the thresher's flail:
And mid these dancing rocks at once and ever
It flung up momently the sacred river.
Five miles meandering with a mazy motion
Through wood and dale the sacred river ran,
Then reached the caverns measureless to man,
And sank in tumult to a lifeless ocean;
And 'mid this tumult Kubla heard from far
Ancestral voices prophesying war!

The shadow of the dome of pleasure
Floated midway on the waves;
Where was heard the mingled measure
From the fountain and the caves.
It was a miracle of rare device,
A sunny pleasure-dome with caves of ice!

A damsel with a dulcimer
In a vision once I saw:
It was an Abyssinian maid
And on her dulcimer she played,
Singing of Mount Abora.
Could I revive within me
Her symphony and song,
To such a deep delight 'twould win me,
That with music loud and long,
I would build that dome in air,
That sunny dome! those caves of ice!
And all who heard should see them there,
And all should cry, Beware! Beware!
His flashing eyes, his floating hair!
Weave a circle round him thrice,
And close your eyes with holy dread
For he on honey-dew hath fed,
And drunk the milk of Paradise.

HART CRANE

My Grandmother's Love Letters

There are no stars tonight
But those of memory.
Yet how much room for memory there is
In the loose girdle of soft rain.

There is even room enough
For the letters of my mother's mother,
Elizabeth,
That have been pressed so long
Into a corner of the roof
That they are brown and soft,
And liable to melt as snow.

Over the greatness of such space
Steps must be gentle.
It is all hung by an invisible white hair.
It trembles as birch limbs webbing the air.

And I ask myself:

"Are your fingers long enough to play
Old keys that are but echoes:
Is the silence strong enough
To carry back the music to its source
And back to you again
As though to her?"

Yet I would lead my grandmother by the hand
Through much of what she would not understand;
And so I stumble. And the rain continues on the roof
With such a sound of gently pitying laughter.

COUNTEE CULLEN

Yet Do I Marvel

I doubt not God is good, well-meaning, kind,
And did He stoop to quibble could tell why
The little buried mole continues blind,
Why flesh that mirrors Him must some day die,
Make plain the reason tortured Tantalus
Is baited by the fickle fruit, declare
If merely brute caprice dooms Sisyphus
To struggle up a never-ending stair.
Inscrutable His ways are, and immune
To catechism by a mind too strewn
With petty cares to slightly understand
What awful brain compels His awful hand.
Yet do I marvel at this curious thing:
To make a poet black, and bid him sing!

E.E. CUMMINGS

---

anyone lived in a pretty how town

anyone lived in a pretty how town
(with up so floating many bells down)
spring summer autumn winter
he sang his didn't he danced his did.

Women and men(both little and small)
cared for anyone not at all
they sowed their isn't they reaped their same
sun moon stars rain

children guessed(but only a few
and down they forgot as up they grew
autumn winter spring summer)
that noone loved him more by more

when by now and tree by leaf
she laughed his joy she cried his grief
bird by snow and stir by still
anyone's any was all to her

someones married their everyones
laughed their cryings and did their dance
(sleep wake hope and then)they
said their nevers they slept their dream

stars rain sun moon
(and only the snow can begin to explain
how children are apt to forget to remember
with up so floating many bells down)

one day anyone died i guess
(and noone stooped to kiss his face)
busy folk buried them side by side
little by little and was by was

all by all and deep by deep
and more by more they dream their sleep
noone and anyone earth by april
wish by spirit and if by yes.

Women and men(both dong and ding)
summer autumn winter spring
reaped their sowing and went their came
sun moon stars rain

TOI DERRICOTTE

Black Boys Play the Classics

The most popular "act" in
Penn Station
is the three black kids in ratty
sneakers & T-shirts playing
two violins and a cello—Brahms.
White men in business suits
have already dug into their pockets
as they pass and they toss in
a dollar or two without stopping.
Brown men in work-soiled khakis
stand with their mouths open,
arms crossed on their bellies
as if they themselves have always
wanted to attempt those bars.
One white boy, three, sits
cross-legged in front of his
idols—in ecstasy—
their slick, dark faces,
their thin, wiry arms,
who must begin to look
like angels!
Why does this trembling
pull us?
A: Beneath the surface we are one.
B: Amazing! I did not think that they could speak this tongue.

EMILY DICKINSON

"Hope" is the thing with feathers

"Hope" is the thing with feathers—
That perches in the soul—
And sings the tune without the words—
And never stops—at all—

And sweetest—in the Gale—is heard—
And sore must be the storm—
That could abash the little Bird—
That kept so many warm—

I've heard it in the chillest land—
And on the strangest Sea—
Yet, never, in Extremity,
It asked a crumb of Me.

I heard a Fly buzz—when I died

I heard a Fly buzz—when I died—
The Stillness in the Room
Was like the Stillness in the Air—
Between the Heaves of Storm—

The Eyes around—had wrung them dry—
And Breaths were gathering firm
For that last Onset—when the King
Be witnessed—in the Room—

I willed my Keepsakes—Signed away
What portion of me be
Assignable—and then it was
There interposed a Fly—

With Blue—uncertain stumbling Buzz—
Between the light—and me—
And then the Windows failed—and then
I could not see to see—

JOHN DONNE

The Good-Morrow

I wonder, by my troth, what thou and I
Did, till we loved? Were we not weaned till then?
But sucked on country pleasures, childishly?
Or snorted we in the Seven Sleepers' den?
'Twas so; but this, all pleasures fancies be.
If ever any beauty I did see,
Which I desired, and got, 'twas but a dream of thee.

And now good-morrow to our waking souls,
Which watch not one another out of fear;
For love, all love of other sights controls,
And makes one little room an everywhere.
Let sea-discoverers to new worlds have gone,
Let maps to other, worlds on worlds have shown,
Let us possess one world, each hath one, and is one.

My face in thine eye, thine in mine appears,
And true plain hearts do in the faces rest;
Where can we find two better hemispheres,
Without sharp north, without declining west?
Whatever dies, was not mixed equally;
If our two loves be one, or, thou and I
Love so alike, that none do slacken, none can die.

Song

Go and catch a falling star,
   Get with child a mandrake root,
Tell me where all past years are,
   Or who cleft the Devil's foot,
Teach me to hear mermaids singing,
   Or to keep off envy's stinging,
      And find
      What wind
Serves to advance an honest mind.

If thou be'st borne to strange sights,
   Things invisible to see,
Ride ten thousand days and nights,
   Till age snow white hairs on thee,
Thou, when thou return'st, wilt tell me
   All strange wonders that befell thee,
      And swear
      Nowhere
Lives a woman true, and fair.

If thou find'st one, let me know,
   Such a pilgrimage were sweet—
Yet do not, I would not go,
   Though at next door we might meet;
Though she were true, when you met her,
   And last, till you write your letter,
      Yet she
      Will be
False, ere I come, to two, or three.

H.D. (HILDA DOOLITTLE)

Helen

All Greece hates
the still eyes in the white face,
the lustre as of olives
where she stands,
and the white hands.

All Greece reviles
the wan face when she smiles,
hating it deeper still
when it grows wan and white,
remembering past enchantments
and past ills.

Greece sees unmoved,
God's daughter, born of love,
the beauty of cool feet
and slenderest knees,
could love indeed the maid,
only if she were laid,
white ash amid funereal cypresses.

RITA DOVE

The Secret Garden

I was ill, lying on my bed of old papers,
when you came with white rabbits in your arms;
and the doves scattered upwards, flying to mothers,
and the snails sighed under their baggage of stone . . .

Now your tongue grows like celery between us:
Because of our love-cries, cabbage darkens in its nest;
the cauliflower thinks of her pale, plump children
and turns greenish-white in a light like the ocean's.

I was sick, fainting in the smell of teabags,
when you came with tomatoes, a good poetry.
I am being wooed. I am being conquered
by a cliff of limestone that leaves chalk on my breasts.

PAUL LAURENCE DUNBAR

We Wear the Mask

We wear the mask that grins and lies,
It hides our cheeks and shades our eyes,—
This debt we pay to human guile;
With torn and bleeding hearts we smile,
And mouth with myriad subtleties.

Why should the world be overwise,
In counting all our tears and sighs?
Nay, let them only see us, while
    We wear the mask.

We smile, but, O great Christ, our cries
To thee from tortured souls arise.
We sing, but oh the clay is vile
Beneath our feet, and long the mile;
But let the world dream otherwise,
    We wear the mask!

T.S. ELIOT

Preludes

I

The winter evening settles down
With smell of steaks in passageways.
Six o'clock.
The burnt-out ends of smoky days.
And now a gusty shower wraps
The grimy scraps
Of withered leaves about your feet
And newspapers from vacant lots;
The showers beat
On broken blinds and chimney-pots,
And at the corner of the street
A lonely cab-horse steams and stamps.

And then the lighting of the lamps.

II

The morning comes to consciousness
Of faint stale smells of beer
From the sawdust-trampled street
With all its muddy feet that press
To early coffee-stands.
With the other masquerades
That time resumes,
One thinks of all the hands
That are raising dingy shades
In a thousand furnished rooms.

III

You tossed a blanket from the bed,
You lay upon your back, and waited;
You dozed, and watched the night revealing
The thousand sordid images

Of which your soul was constituted;
They flickered against the ceiling.
And when all the world came back
And the light crept up between the shutters
And you heard the sparrows in the gutters,
You had such a vision of the street
As the street hardly understands;
Sitting along the bed's edge, where
You curled the papers from your hair,
Or clasped the yellow soles of feet
In the palms of both soiled hands.

IV

His soul stretched tight across the skies
That fade behind a city block,
Or trampled by insistent feet
At four and five and six o'clock;
And short square fingers stuffing pipes,
And evening newspapers, and eyes
Assured of certain certainties,
The conscience of a blackened street
Impatient to assume the world.

I am moved by fancies that are curled
Around these images, and cling:
The notion of some infinitely gentle
Infinitely suffering thing.

Wipe your hand across your mouth, and laugh;
The worlds revolve like ancient women
Gathering fuel in vacant lots.

QUEEN ELIZABETH I

When I was Fair and Young

When I was fair and young, then favor graced me.
Of many was I sought their mistress for to be.
But I did scorn them all and answered them therefore:
Go, go, go, seek some other where; importune me no more.

How many weeping eyes I made to pine in woe,
How many sighing hearts I have not skill to show,
But I the prouder grew and still this spake therefore:
Go, go, go, seek some other where, importune me no more.

Then spake fair Venus' son, that proud victorious boy,
Saying: You dainty dame, for that you be so coy,
I will so pluck your plumes as you shall say no more:
Go, go, go, seek some other where, importune me no more.

As soon as he had said, such change grew in my breast
That neither night nor day I could take any rest.
Wherefore I did repent that I had said before:
Go, go, go, seek some other where, importune me no more.

RALPH WALDO EMERSON

Concord Hymn

Sung at the Completion of the Battle Monument, July 4, 1837

By the rude bridge that arched the flood,
    Their flag to April's breeze unfurled,
Here once the embattled farmers stood
    And fired the shot heard round the world.

The foe long since in silence slept;
    Alike the conqueror silent sleeps;
And Time the ruined bridge has swept
    Down the dark stream which seaward creeps.

On this green bank, by this soft stream,
    We set today a votive stone;
That memory may their deed redeem,
    When, like our sires, our sons are gone.

Spirit, that made those heroes dare
    To die, and leave their children free,
Bid Time and Nature gently spare
    The shaft we raise to them and thee.

RHINA P. ESPAILLAT

Bilingual/Bilingüe

My father liked them separate, one there,
one here (allá y aquí), as if aware

that words might cut in two his daughter's heart
(el corazón) and lock the alien part

to what he was—his memory, his name
(su nombre)—with a key he could not claim.

"English outside this door, Spanish inside,"
he said, "y basta." But who can divide

the world, the word (mundo y palabra) from
any child? I knew how to be dumb

and stubborn (testaruda); late, in bed,
I hoarded secret syllables I read

until my tongue (mi lengua) learned to run
where his stumbled. And still the heart was one.

I like to think he knew that, even when,
proud (orgulloso) of his daughter's pen,

he stood outside mis versos, half in fear
of words he loved but wanted not to hear.

ANNE FINCH, COUNTESS OF WINCHILSEA

Adam Posed

Could our first father, at his toilsome plow,
Thorns in his path, and labor on his brow,
Clothed only in a rude, unpolished skin,
Could he a vain fantastic nymph have seen,
In all her airs, in all her antic graces,
Her various fashions, and more various faces;
How had it posed that skill, which late assigned
Just appellations to each several kind!
A right idea of the sight to frame;
T'have guessed from what new element she came;
T'have hit the wavering form, or given this thing a name.

ROBERT FROST

The Road Not Taken

Two roads diverged in a yellow wood,
And sorry I could not travel both
And be one traveler, long I stood
And looked down one as far as I could
To where it bent in the undergrowth;

Then took the other, as just as fair,
And having perhaps the better claim,
Because it was grassy and wanted wear;
Though as for that the passing there
Had worn them really about the same,

And both that morning equally lay
In leaves no step had trodden black.
Oh, I kept the first for another day!
Yet knowing how way leads on to way,
I doubted if I should ever come back.

I shall be telling this with a sigh
Somewhere ages and ages hence:
Two roads diverged in a wood, and I—
I took the one less traveled by,
And that has made all the difference.

Fire and Ice

Some say the world will end in fire,
Some say in ice.
From what I've tasted of desire
I hold with those who favor fire.
But if it had to perish twice,
I think I know enough of hate
To say that for destruction ice
Is also great
And would suffice.

Stopping by Woods on a Snowy Evening

Whose woods these are I think I know.
His house is in the village though;
He will not see me stopping here
To watch his woods fill up with snow.

My little horse must think it queer
To stop without a farmhouse near
Between the woods and frozen lake
The darkest evening of the year.

He gives his harness bells a shake
To ask if there is some mistake.
The only other sound's the sweep
Of easy wind and downy flake.

The woods are lovely, dark and deep.
But I have promises to keep,
And miles to go before I sleep,
And miles to go before I sleep.

THOMAS GRAY

Ode on the Death of a Favourite Cat, Drowned in a Tub of Goldfishes

'Twas on a lofty vase's side,
Where China's gayest art had dyed
    The azure flowers that blow;
Demurest of the tabby kind,
The pensive Selima, reclined,
    Gazed on the lake below.

Her conscious tail her joy declared;
The fair round face, the snowy beard,
    The velvet of her paws,
Her coat, that with the tortoise vies,
Her ears of jet, and emerald eyes,
    She saw; and purred applause.

Still had she gazed; but 'midst the tide
Two angel forms were seen to glide,
    The genii of the stream;
Their scaly armour's Tyrian hue
Through richest purple to the view
    Betrayed a golden gleam.

The hapless nymph with wonder saw;
A whisker first and then a claw,
    With many an ardent wish,
She stretched in vain to reach the prize.
What female heart can gold despise?
    What cat's averse to fish?

Presumptuous maid! with looks intent
Again she stretch'd, again she bent,
    Nor knew the gulf between.
(Malignant Fate sat by, and smiled)
The slippery verge her feet beguiled,
    She tumbled headlong in.

Eight times emerging from the flood
She mewed to every watery god,
    Some speedy aid to send.
No dolphin came, no Nereid stirred;
Nor cruel Tom, nor Susan heard;
    A Favourite has no friend!

From hence, ye beauties, undeceived,
Know, one false step is ne'er retrieved,
    And be with caution bold.
Not all that tempts your wandering eyes
And heedless hearts, is lawful prize;
    Nor all that glisters, gold.

THOMAS HARDY

Channel Firing

That night your great guns, unawares,
Shook all our coffins as we lay,
And broke the chancel window-squares,
We thought it was the Judgment-day

And sat upright. While drearisome
Arose the howl of wakened hounds;
The mouse let fall the altar-crumb,
The worms drew back into the mounds,

The glebe cow drooled. Till God called, "No;
It's gunnery practice out at sea
Just as before you went below;
The world is as it used to be;

"All nations striving strong to make
Red war yet redder. Mad as hatters
They do no more for Christés sake
Than you who are helpless in such matters.

"That this is not the judgment-hour
For some of them's a blessed thing,
For if it were they'd have to scour
Hell's floor for so much threatening. . . .

"Ha, ha. It will be warmer when
I blow the trumpet (if indeed
I ever do; for you are men,
And rest eternal sorely need)."

So down we lay again. "I wonder,
Will the world ever saner be,"
Said one, "than when He sent us under
In our indifferent century!"

And many a skeleton shook his head.
"Instead of preaching forty year,"
My neighbour Parson Thirdly said,
"I wish I had stuck to pipes and beer."

Again the guns disturbed the hour,
Roaring their readiness to avenge,
As far inland as Stourton Tower,
And Camelot, and starlit Stonehenge.

JOY HARJO

Eagle Poem

To pray you open your whole self
To sky, to earth, to sun, to moon
To one whole voice that is you.
And know there is more
That you can't see, can't hear;
Can't know except in moments
Steadly growing, and in languages
That aren't always sound but other
Circles of motion.
Like eagle that Sunday morning
Over Salt River. Circled in blue sky
In wind, swept our hearts clean
With sacred wings.
We see you, see ourselves and know
That we must take the utmost care
And kindness in all things.
Breathe in, knowing we are made of
All this, and breathe, knowing
We are truly blessed because we
Were born, and die soon within a
True circle of motion,
Like eagle rounding out the morning
Inside us.
We pray that it will be done
In beauty.
In beauty.

MICHAEL S. HARPER

Grandfather

In 1915 my grandfather's
neighbors surrounded his house
near the dayline he ran
on the Hudson
in Catskill, NY
and thought they'd burn
his family out
in a movie they'd just seen
and be rid of his kind:
the death of a lone black
family is *the Birth
of a Nation*,
or so they thought.
His 5'4" waiter gait
quenched the white jacket smile
he'd brought back from watered
polish of my father
on the turning seats,
and he asked his neighbors
up on his thatched porch
for the first blossom of fire
that would bring him down.
They went away, his nation,
spittooning their torched necks
in the shadows of the riverboat
they'd seen, posse decomposing;
and I see him on Sutter
with white bag from your
restaurant, challenged by his first
grandson to a foot-race
he will win in white clothes.

I see him as he buys galoshes
for his railed yard near Mineo's

metal shop, where roses jump
as the el circles his house
toward Brooklyn, where his rain fell;
and I see cigar smoke in his eyes,
chocolate Madison Square Garden chews
he breaks on his set teeth,
stitched up after cancer,
the great white nation immovable
as his weight wilts
and he is on a porch
that won't hold my arms,
or the legs of the race run
forwards, or the film
played backwards on his grandson's eyes.

ROBERT HAYDEN

Those Winter Sundays

Sundays too my father got up early
and put his clothes on in the blueblack cold,
then with cracked hands that ached
from labor in the weekday weather made
banked fires blaze. No one ever thanked him.

I'd wake and hear the cold splintering, breaking.
When the rooms were warm, he'd call,
and slowly I would rise and dress,
fearing the chronic angers of that house,

Speaking indifferently to him,
who had driven out the cold
and polished my good shoes as well.
What did I know, what did I know
of love's austere and lonely offices?

GEORGE HERBERT

The Pulley

When God at first made man,
Having a glass of blessings standing by,
"Let us," said he, "pour on him all we can.
Let the world's riches, which dispersèd lie,
   Contract into a span."

So strength first made a way;
Then beauty flowed, then wisdom, honour, pleasure.
When almost all was out, God made a stay,
Perceiving that, alone of all his treasure,
   Rest in the bottom lay.

"For if I should," said he,
"Bestow this jewel also on my creature,
He would adore my gifts instead of me,
And rest in Nature, not the God of Nature;
   So both should losers be.

"Yet let him keep the rest,
But keep them with repining restlessness;
Let him be rich and weary, that at least,
If goodness lead him not, yet weariness
   May toss him to my breast."

ROBERT HERRICK

To the Virgins, to Make Much of Time

Gather ye rose-buds while ye may,
    Old Time is still a-flying;
And this same flower that smiles today
    Tomorrow will be dying.

The glorious lamp of heaven, the sun,
    The higher he's a-getting,
The sooner will his race be run,
    And nearer he's to setting.

That age is best which is the first,
    When youth and blood are warmer;
But being spent, the worse, and worst
    Times still succeed the former.

Then be not coy, but use your time,
    And while ye may, go marry;
For having lost but once your prime,
    You may forever tarry.

OLIVER WENDELL HOLMES

Old Ironsides

Ay, tear her tattered ensign down!
  Long has it waved on high,
And many an eye has danced to see
  That banner in the sky;
Beneath it rung the battle shout,
  And burst the cannon's roar;—
The meteor of the ocean air
  Shall sweep the clouds no more!

Her deck, once red with heroes' blood
  Where knelt the vanquished foe,
When winds were hurrying o'er the flood
  And waves were white below,
No more shall feel the victor's tread,
  Or know the conquered knee;—
The harpies of the shore shall pluck
  The eagle of the sea!

O, better that her shattered hulk
  Should sink beneath the wave;
Her thunders shook the mighty deep,
  And there should be her grave;
Nail to the mast her holy flag,
  Set every thread-bare sail,
And give her to the god of storms,—
  The lightning and the gale!

GERARD MANLEY HOPKINS

Pied Beauty

Glory be to God for dappled things—
  For skies of couple-colour as a brinded cow;
    For rose-moles all in stipple upon trout that swim;
Fresh-firecoal chestnut-falls; finches' wings;
  Landscape plotted and pieced—fold, fallow, and plough;
    And áll trádes, their gear and tackle and trim.

All things counter, original, spare, strange;
  Whatever is fickle, freckled (who knows how?)
    With swift, slow; sweet, sour; adazzle, dim;
He fathers-forth whose beauty is past change:
        Praise him.

A.E. HOUSMAN

To an Athlete Dying Young

The time you won your town the race
We chaired you through the market-place;
Man and boy stood cheering by,
And home we brought you shoulder-high.

Today, the road all runners come,
Shoulder-high we bring you home,
And set you at your threshold down,
Townsman of a stiller town.

Smart lad, to slip betimes away
From fields where glory does not stay,
And early though the laurel grows
It withers quicker than the rose.

Eyes the shady night has shut
Cannot see the record cut,
And silence sounds no worse than cheers
After earth has stopped the ears.

Now you will not swell the rout
Of lads that wore their honours out,
Runners whom renown outran
And the name died before the man.

So set, before its echoes fade,
The fleet foot on the sill of shade,
And hold to the low lintel up
The still-defended challenge-cup.

And round that early-laurelled head
Will flock to gaze the strengthless dead,
And find unwithered on its curls
The garland briefer than a girl's.

JULIA WARD HOWE

Battle-Hymn of the Republic

Mine eyes have seen the glory of the coming of the Lord:
He is trampling out the vintage where the grapes of wrath are stored;
He hath loosed the fatal lightning of his terrible swift sword:
    His truth is marching on.

I have seen Him in the watch-fires of a hundred circling camps;
They have builded Him an altar in the evening dews and damps;
I can read His righteous sentence by the dim and flaring lamps.
    His Day is marching on.

I have read a fiery gospel, writ in burnished rows of steel:
"As ye deal with my contemners, so with you my grace shall deal;
Let the Hero, born of woman, crush the serpent with his heel,
    Since God is marching on."

He has sounded forth the trumpet that shall never call retreat;
He is sifting out the hearts of men before his judgment-seat:
Oh! be swift, my soul, to answer Him! be jubilant, my feet!
    Our God is marching on.

In the beauty of the lilies Christ was born across the sea,
With a glory in his bosom that transfigures you and me:
As he died to make men holy, let us die to make men free,
    While God is marching on.

MARY HOWITT

The Spider and the Fly

"Will you walk into my parlour?" said the Spider to the Fly,
'Tis the prettiest little parlour that ever you did spy;
The way into my parlour is up a winding stair,
And I've a many curious things to shew when you are there."
"Oh no, no," said the little Fly, "to ask me is in vain,
For who goes up your winding stair can ne'er come down again."

"I'm sure you must be weary, dear, with soaring up so high;
Will you rest upon my little bed?" said the Spider to the Fly.
"There are pretty curtains drawn around; the sheets are fine and thin,
And if you like to rest awhile, I'll snugly tuck you in!"
"Oh no, no," said the little Fly, "for I've often heard it said,
They never, never wake again, who sleep upon your bed!"

Said the cunning Spider to the Fly, "Dear friend what can I do,
To prove the warm affection I've always felt for you?
I have within my pantry, good store of all that's nice;
I'm sure you're very welcome—will you please to take a slice?"
"Oh no, no," said the little Fly, "kind Sir, that cannot be,
I've heard what's in your pantry, and I do not wish to see!"

"Sweet creature!" said the Spider, "you're witty and you're wise,
How handsome are your gauzy wings, how brilliant are your eyes!
I've a little looking-glass upon my parlour shelf,
If you'll step in one moment, dear, you shall behold yourself."
"I thank you, gentle Sir," she said, "for what you're pleased to say,
And bidding you good morning now, I'll call another day."

The Spider turned him round about, and went into his den,
For well he knew the silly Fly would soon come back again:
So he wove a subtle web, in a little corner sly,
And set his table ready, to dine upon the Fly.

Then he came out to his door again, and merrily did sing,
"Come hither, hither, pretty Fly, with the pearl and silver wing;
Your robes are green and purple—there's a crest upon your head;
Your eyes are like the diamond bright, but mine are dull as lead!"

Alas, alas! how very soon this silly little Fly,
Hearing his wily, flattering words, came slowly flitting by;
With buzzing wings she hung aloft, then near and nearer drew,
Thinking only of her brilliant eyes, and green and purple hue—
Thinking only of her crested head—poor foolish thing! At last,
Up jumped the cunning Spider, and fiercely held her fast.
He dragged her up his winding stair, into his dismal den,
Within his little parlour—but she ne'er came out again!

And now dear little children, who may this story read,
To idle, silly flattering words, I pray you ne'er give heed:
Unto an evil counsellor, close heart and ear and eye,
And take a lesson from this tale, of the Spider and the Fly.

LANGSTON HUGHES

Harlem

What happens to a dream deferred?

 Does it dry up
like a raisin in the sun?
Or fester like a sore—
And then run?
Does it stink like rotten meat?
Or crust and sugar over—
like a syrupy sweet?

Maybe it just sags
like a heavy load.

Or does it explode?

JAMES WELDON JOHNSON

Lift Ev'ry Voice and Sing

Lift ev'ry voice and sing,
Till earth and heaven ring,
Ring with the harmonies of Liberty;
Let our rejoicing rise
High as the list'ning skies,
Let it resound loud as the rolling sea.
Sing a song full of the faith that the dark past has taught us,
Sing a song full of the hope that the present has brought us;
Facing the rising sun of our new day begun,
Let us march on till victory is won.

Stony the road we trod,
Bitter the chast'ning rod,
Felt in the days when hope unborn had died;
Yet with a steady beat,
Have not our weary feet
Come to the place for which our fathers sighed?
We have come over a way that with tears has been watered,
We have come, treading our path through the blood of the slaughtered,
Out from the gloomy past,
Till now we stand at last
Where the white gleam of our bright star is cast.

God of our weary years,
God of our silent tears,
Thou who has brought us thus far on the way;
Thou who has by Thy might,
Led us into the light,
Keep us forever in the path, we pray.
Lest our feet stray from the places, our God, where we met Thee,
Lest our hearts, drunk with the wine of the world, we forget Thee;
Shadowed beneath Thy hand,
May we forever stand,
True to our God,
True to our native land.

BEN JONSON

Song to Celia

Drink to me only with thine eyes,
    And I will pledge with mine;
Or leave a kiss but in the cup,
    And I'll not ask for wine.
The thirst that from the soul doth rise
    Doth ask a drink divine;
But might I of Jove's nectar sup,
    I would not change for thine.

I sent thee late a rosy wreath,
    Not so much honouring thee
As giving it a hope that there
    It could not withered be;
But thou thereon didst only breathe,
    And sent'st it back to me;
Since when it grows, and smells, I swear,
    Not of itself but thee.

JOHN KEATS

When I Have Fears That I May Cease to Be

When I have fears that I may cease to be
   Before my pen has gleaned my teeming brain,
Before high-pilèd books, in charactery,
   Hold like rich garners the full ripened grain;
When I behold, upon the night's starred face,
   Huge cloudy symbols of a high romance,
And think that I may never live to trace
   Their shadows with the magic hand of chance;
And when I feel, fair creature of an hour,
   That I shall never look upon thee more,
Never have relish in the fairy power
   Of unreflecting love—then on the shore
Of the wide world I stand alone, and think
Till love and fame to nothingness do sink.

La Belle Dame sans Merci: A Ballad

Ah, what can ail thee, knight-at-arms,
  Alone and palely loitering?
The sedge has withered from the lake,
  And no birds sing.

O what can ail thee, knight-at-arms,
  So haggard and so woe-begone?
The squirrel's granary is full,
  And the harvest's done.

I see a lily on thy brow,
  With anguish moist and fever-dew,
And on thy cheeks a fading rose
  Fast withereth too.

I met a lady in the meads
  Full beautiful, a fairy's child;
Her hair was long, her foot was light,
  And her eyes were wild.

I made a garland for her head,
  And bracelets too, and fragrant zone;
She looked at me as she did love,
  And made sweet moan.

I set her on my pacing steed,
  And nothing else saw all day long,
For sidelong would she bend, and sing
  A fairy's song.

She found me roots of relish sweet,
  And honey wild, and manna-dew;
And sure in language strange she said—
  'I love thee true.'

She took me to her elfin grot,
   And there she wept and sighed full sore,
And there I shut her wild wild eyes
   With kisses four.

And there she lulled me asleep,
   And there I dreamed—Ah! woe betide!
The latest dream I ever dreamt
   On the cold hill's side.

I saw pale kings and princes too,
   Pale warriors, death-pale were they all;
They cried—'La Belle Dame sans Merci
   Hath thee in thrall!'

I saw their starved lips in the gloam
   With horrid warning gaped wide,
And I awoke and found me here
   On the cold hill's side.

And this is why I sojourn here,
   Alone and palely loitering,
Though the sedge is withered from the lake,
   And no birds sing.

JOYCE KILMER

Trees

For Mrs. Henry Mills Alden

I think that I shall never see
A poem lovely as a tree.

A tree whose hungry mouth is prest
Against the earth's sweet flowing breast;

A tree that looks at God all day,
And lifts her leafy arms to pray;

A tree that may in Summer wear
A nest of robins in her hair;

Upon whose bosom snow has lain;
Who intimately lives with rain.

Poems are made by fools like me,
But only God can make a tree.

YUSEF KOMUNYAKAA

Kindness

For Carol Rigolot

I acknowledge my status as a stranger:
    When deeds splay before us
precious as gold & unused chances
stripped from the whine-bone,
we know the moment kindheartedness
walks in. Each *praise be*
echoes us back as the years uncount
themselves, eating salt. Though blood
first shaped us on the climbing wheel,
the human mind lit by the savanna's
ice star & thistle rose,
your knowing gaze enters a room
& opens the day,
saying we were made for fun.
Even the bedazzled brute knows
when sunlight falls through leaves
across honed knives on the table.
If we can see it push shadows
aside, growing closer, are we less
broken? A barometer, temperature
gauge, a ruler in minus fractions
& pedigrees, a thingmajig,
a probe with an all-seeing eye,
what do we need to measure
kindness, every unheld breath,
every unkind leapyear?
Sometimes a sober voice is enough
to calm the waters & drive away
the false witnesses, saying, Look,
here are the broken treaties Beauty
brought to us earthbound sentinels.

EMMA LAZARUS

The New Colossus

Not like the brazen giant of Greek fame,
With conquering limbs astride from land to land;
Here at our sea-washed, sunset gates shall stand
A mighty woman with a torch, whose flame
Is the imprisoned lightning, and her name
Mother of Exiles. From her beacon-hand
Glows world-wide welcome; her mild eyes command
The air-bridged harbor that twin cities frame.
"Keep, ancient lands, your storied pomp!" cries she
With silent lips. "Give me your tired, your poor,
Your huddled masses yearning to breathe free,
The wretched refuse of your teeming shore.
Send these, the homeless, tempest-tost to me,
I lift my lamp beside the golden door!"

EDWARD LEAR

The Owl and the Pussy-Cat

I

The Owl and the Pussy-Cat went to sea
    In a beautiful pea-green boat,
They took some honey, and plenty of money,
    Wrapped up in a five-pound note.
The Owl looked up to the stars above,
    And sang to a small guitar,
'O lovely Pussy, O Pussy, my love,
    What a beautiful Pussy you are,
        You are,
        You are!
What a beautiful Pussy you are!'

II

Pussy said to the Owl, 'You elegant fowl!
    How charmingly sweet you sing!
O let us be married! too long we have tarried:
    But what shall we do for a ring?'
They sailed away, for a year and a day,
    To the land where the Bong-tree grows
And there in a wood a Piggy-wig stood,
    With a ring at the end of his nose,
        His nose,
        His nose,
With a ring at the end of his nose.

III

'Dear Pig, are you willing to sell for one shilling
    Your ring?' Said the Piggy, 'I will.'
So they took it away, and were married next day
    By the Turkey who lives on the hill.

They dined on mince, and slices of quince,
　　Which they ate with a runcible spoon;
And hand in hand, on the edge of the sand,
　　They danced by the light of the moon,
　　　　The moon,
　　　　The moon,
They danced by the light of the moon.

LI-YOUNG LEE

The Gift

To pull the metal splinter from my palm
my father recited a story in a low voice.
I watched his lovely face and not the blade.
Before the story ended, he'd removed
the iron sliver I thought I'd die from.

I can't remember the tale,
but hear his voice still, a well
of dark water, a prayer.
And I recall his hands,
two measures of tenderness
he laid against my face,
the flames of discipline
he raised above my head.

Had you entered that afternoon
you would have thought you saw a man
planting something in a boy's palm,
a silver tear, a tiny flame.
Had you followed that boy
you would have arrived here,
where I bend over my wife's right hand.

Look how I shave her thumbnail down
so carefully she feels no pain.
Watch as I lift the splinter out.
I was seven when my father
took my hand like this,
and I did not hold that shard
between my fingers and think,
Metal that will bury me,
christen it Little Assassin,
Ore Going Deep for My Heart.

And I did not lift up my wound and cry,
Death visited here!
I did what a child does
when he's given something to keep.
I kissed my father.

SHIRLEY GEOK-LIN LIM

Learning to Love America

because it has no pure products

because the Pacific Ocean sweeps along the coastline
because the water of the ocean is cold
and because land is better than ocean

because I say we rather than they

because I live in California
I have eaten fresh artichokes
and jacaranda bloom in April and May

because my senses have caught up with my body
my breath with the air it swallows
my hunger with my mouth

because I walk barefoot in my house

because I have nursed my son at my breast
because he is a strong American boy
because I have seen his eyes redden when he is asked who he is
because he answers I don't know

because to have a son is to have a country
because my son will bury me here
because countries are in our blood and we bleed them

because it is late and too late to change my mind
because it is time.

VACHEL LINDSAY

General William Booth Enters Into Heaven

[BASS DRUM BEATEN LOUDLY]
Booth led boldly with his big bass drum—
(Are you washed in the blood of the Lamb?)
The Saints smiled gravely and they said: "He's come."
(Are you washed in the blood of the Lamb?)
Walking lepers followed, rank on rank,
Lurching bravoes from the ditches dank,
Drabs from the alleyways and drug fiends pale—
Minds still passion-ridden, soul-powers frail:—
Vermin-eaten saints with mouldy breath,
Unwashed legions with the ways of Death—
(Are you washed in the blood of the Lamb?)

[BANJOS]
Every slum had sent its half-a-score
The round world over. (Booth had groaned for more.)
Every banner that the wide world flies
Bloomed with glory and transcendent dyes.
Big-voiced lasses made their banjos bang,
Tranced, fanatical they shrieked and sang:—
"Are you washed in the blood of the Lamb?"
Hallelujah! It was queer to see
Bull-necked convicts with that land make free.
Loons with trumpets blowed a blare, blare, blare
On, on upward thro' the golden air!
(Are you washed in the blood of the Lamb?)

[BASS DRUM SLOWER AND SOFTER]
Booth died blind and still by Faith he trod,
Eyes still dazzled by the ways of God.
Booth led boldly, and he looked the chief
Eagle countenance in sharp relief,
Beard a-flying, air of high command
Unabated in that holy land.

[SWEET FLUTE MUSIC]
Jesus came from out the court-house door,
Stretched his hands above the passing poor.
Booth saw not, but led his queer ones there
Round and round the mighty court-house square.
Yet in an instant all that blear review
Marched on spotless, clad in raiment new.
The lame were straightened, withered limbs uncurled
And blind eyes opened on a new, sweet world.

[BASS DRUM LOUDER]
Drabs and vixens in a flash made whole!
Gone was the weasel-head, the snout, the jowl!
Sages and sibyls now, and athletes clean,
Rulers of empires, and of forests green!

[GRAND CHORUS OF ALL INSTRUMENTS.
TAMBOURINES TO THE FOREGROUND]
The hosts were sandalled, and their wings were fire!
(Are you washed in the blood of the Lamb?)
But their noise played havoc with the angel-choir.
(Are you washed in the blood of the Lamb?)
O shout Salvation! It was good to see
Kings and Princes by the Lamb set free.
The banjos rattled and the tambourines
Jing-jing-jingled in the hands of Queens.

[REVERENTLY SUNG. NO INSTRUMENTS]
And when Booth halted by the curb for prayer
He saw his Master thro' the flag-filled air.
Christ came gently with a robe and crown
For Booth the soldier, while the throng knelt down.
He saw King Jesus. They were face to face,
And he knelt a-weeping in that holy place.
Are you washed in the blood of the Lamb?

HENRY WADSWORTH LONGFELLOW

A Psalm of Life

What the Heart of the Young Man
Said to the Psalmist

Tell me not, in mournful numbers,
    Life is but an empty dream!
For the soul is dead that slumbers,
    And things are not what they seem.

Life is real! Life is earnest!
    And the grave is not its goal;
Dust thou art, to dust returnest,
    Was not spoken of the soul.

Not enjoyment, and not sorrow,
    Is our destined end or way;
But to act, that each to-morrow
    Find us farther than to-day.

Art is long, and Time is fleeting,
    And our hearts, though stout and brave,
Still, like muffled drums, are beating
    Funeral marches to the grave.

In the world's broad field of battle,
    In the bivouac of Life,
Be not like dumb, driven cattle!
    Be a hero in the strife!

Trust no Future, howe'er pleasant!
    Let the dead Past bury its dead!
Act,— act in the living Present!
    Heart within, and God o'erhead!

Lives of great men all remind us
  We can make our lives sublime,
And, departing, leave behind us
  Footprints on the sands of time;

Footprints, that perhaps another,
  Sailing o'er life's solemn main,
A forlorn and shipwrecked brother,
  Seeing, shall take heart again.

Let us, then, be up and doing,
  With a heart for any fate;
Still achieving, still pursuing,
  Learn to labor and to wait.

RICHARD LOVELACE

To Althea, from Prison

When Love with unconfinèd wings
    Hovers within my Gates,
And my divine *Althea* brings
    To whisper at the Grates;
When I lie tangled in her hair,
    And fettered to her eye,
The Gods that wanton in the Air,
    Know no such Liberty.

When flowing Cups run swiftly round
    With no allaying *Thames*,
Our careless heads with Roses bound,
    Our hearts with Loyal Flames;
When thirsty grief in Wine we steep,
    When Healths and draughts go free,
Fishes that tipple in the Deep
    Know no such Liberty.

When (like committed linnets) I
    With shriller throat shall sing
The sweetness, Mercy, Majesty,
    And glories of my King;
When I shall voice aloud how good
    He is, how Great should be,
Enlargèd Winds, that curl the Flood,
    Know no such Liberty.

Stone Walls do not a Prison make,
    Nor Iron bars a Cage;
Minds innocent and quiet take
    That for an Hermitage.
If I have freedom in my Love,
    And in my soul am free,
Angels alone that soar above,
    Enjoy such Liberty.

CHRISTOPHER MARLOWE

The Passionate Shepherd to His Love

Come live with me and be my love,
And we will all the pleasures prove,
That Valleys, groves, hills, and fields,
Woods, or steepy mountain yields.

And we will sit upon the Rocks,
Seeing the Shepherds feed their flocks,
By shallow Rivers to whose falls
Melodious birds sing Madrigals.

And I will make thee beds of Roses
And a thousand fragrant posies,
A cap of flowers, and a kirtle
Embroidered all with leaves of Myrtle;

A gown made of the finest wool
Which from our pretty Lambs we pull;
Fair lined slippers for the cold,
With buckles of the purest gold;

A belt of straw and Ivy buds,
With Coral clasps and Amber studs:
And if these pleasures may thee move,
Come live with me, and be my love.

The Shepherds' Swains shall dance and sing
For thy delight each May-morning:
If these delights thy mind may move,
Then live with me, and be my love.

ANDREW MARVELL

To His Coy Mistress

Had we but world enough and time,
This coyness, lady, were no crime.
We would sit down, and think which way
To walk, and pass our long love's day.
Thou by the Indian Ganges' side
Shouldst rubies find; I by the tide
Of Humber would complain. I would
Love you ten years before the flood,
And you should, if you please, refuse
Till the conversion of the Jews.
My vegetable love should grow
Vaster than empires and more slow;
An hundred years should go to praise
Thine eyes, and on thy forehead gaze;
Two hundred to adore each breast,
But thirty thousand to the rest;
An age at least to every part,
And the last age should show your heart.
For, lady, you deserve this state,
Nor would I love at lower rate.

      But at my back I always hear
Time's wingèd chariot hurrying near;
And yonder all before us lie
Deserts of vast eternity.
Thy beauty shall no more be found;
Nor, in thy marble vault, shall sound
My echoing song; then worms shall try
That long-preserved virginity,
And your quaint honour turn to dust,
And into ashes all my lust;
The grave's a fine and private place,
But none, I think, do there embrace.

Now therefore, while the youthful hue
Sits on thy skin like morning dew,
And while thy willing soul transpires
At every pore with instant fires,
Now let us sport us while we may,
And now, like amorous birds of prey,
Rather at once our time devour
Than languish in his slow-chapped power.
Let us roll all our strength and all
Our sweetness up into one ball,
And tear our pleasures with rough strife
Thorough the iron gates of life:
Thus, though we cannot make our sun
Stand still, yet we will make him run.

DAVID MASON

Song of the Powers

Mine, said the stone,
mine is the hour.
I crush the scissors,
such is my power.
Stronger than wishes,
my power, alone.

Mine, said the paper,
mine are the words
that smother the stone
with imagined birds,
reams of them, flown
from the mind of the shaper.

Mine, said the scissors,
mine all the knives
gashing through paper's
ethereal lives;
nothing's so proper
as tattering wishes.

As stone crushes scissors,
as paper snuffs stone
and scissors cut paper,
all end alone.
So heap up your paper
and scissor your wishes
and uproot the stone
from the top of the hill.
They all end alone
as you will, you will.

Mrs. Kessler

Mr. Kessler, you know, was in the army,
And he drew six dollars a month as a pension,
And stood on the corner talking politics,
Or sat at home reading Grant's *Memoirs*;
And I supported the family by washing,
Learning the secrets of all the people
From their curtains, counterpanes, shirts and skirts.
For things that are new grow old at length,
They're replaced with better or none at all:
People are prospering or falling back.
And rents and patches widen with time;
No thread or needle can pace decay,
And there are stains that baffle soap,
And there are colors that run in spite of you,
Blamed though you are for spoiling a dress.
Handkerchiefs, napery, have their secrets—
The laundress, Life, knows all about it.
And I, who went to all the funerals
Held in Spoon River, swear I never
Saw a dead face without thinking it looked
Like something washed and ironed.

CLAUDE McKAY

Romance

To clasp you now and feel your head close-pressed,
Scented and warm against my beating breast;

To whisper soft and quivering your name,
And drink the passion burning in your frame;

To lie at full length, taut, with cheek to cheek,
And tease your mouth with kisses till you speak

Love words, mad words, dream words, sweet senseless words,
Melodious like notes of mating birds;

To hear you ask if I shall love always,
And myself answer: Till the end of days;

To feel your easeful sigh of happiness
When on your trembling lips I murmur: Yes;

It is so sweet. We know it is not true.
What matters it? The night must shed her dew.

We know it is not true, but it is sweet—
The poem with this music is complete.

HERMAN MELVILLE

The Maldive Shark

About the Shark, phlegmatical one,
Pale sot of the Maldive sea,
The sleek little pilot-fish, azure and slim,
How alert in attendance be.
From his saw-pit of mouth, from his charnel of maw
They have nothing of harm to dread,
But liquidly glide on his ghastly flank
Or before his Gorgonian head;
Or lurk in the port of serrated teeth
In white triple tiers of glittering gates,
And there find a haven when peril's abroad,
An asylum in jaws of the Fates!

They are friends; and friendly they guide him to prey,
Yet never partake of the treat—
Eyes and brains to the dotard lethargic and dull,
Pale ravener of horrible meat.

EDNA ST. VINCENT MILLAY

I think I should have loved you presently

I think I should have loved you presently,
And given in earnest words I flung in jest;
And lifted honest eyes for you to see,
And caught your hand against my cheek and breast;
And all my pretty follies flung aside
That won you to me, and beneath your gaze,
Naked of reticence and shorn of pride,
Spread like a chart my little wicked ways.
I, that had been to you, had you remained,
But one more waking from a recurrent dream,
Cherish no less the certain stakes I gained,
And walk your memory's halls, austere, supreme,
A ghost in marble of a girl you knew
Who would have loved you in a day or two.

What lips my lips have kissed, and where, and why

What lips my lips have kissed, and where, and why,
I have forgotten, and what arms have lain
Under my head till morning; but the rain
Is full of ghosts tonight, that tap and sigh
Upon the glass and listen for reply,
And in my heart there stirs a quiet pain
For unremembered lads that not again
Will turn to me at midnight with a cry.
Thus in the winter stands the lonely tree,
Nor knows what birds have vanished one by one,
Yet knows its boughs more silent than before:
I cannot say what loves have come and gone,
I only know that summer sang in me
A little while, that in me sings no more.

JOHN MILTON

When I consider how my light is spent

When I consider how my light is spent,
    Ere half my days, in this dark world and wide,
    And that one Talent which is death to hide
    Lodged with me useless, though my Soul more bent
To serve therewith my Maker, and present
    My true account, lest he returning chide;
    "Doth God exact day-labour, light denied?"
    I fondly ask. But patience, to prevent
That murmur, soon replies, "God doth not need
    Either man's work or his own gifts; who best
    Bear his mild yoke, they serve him best. His state
Is Kingly. Thousands at his bidding speed
    And post o'er Land and Ocean without rest:
    They also serve who only stand and wait."

N. SCOTT MOMADAY

The Delight Song of Tsoai-talee

I am a feather on the bright sky
I am the blue horse that runs in the plain
I am the fish that rolls, shining, in the water
I am the shadow that follows a child
I am the evening light, the lustre of meadows
I am an eagle playing with the wind
I am a cluster of bright beads
I am the farthest star
I am the cold of dawn
I am the roaring of the rain
I am the glitter on the crust of the snow
I am the long track of the moon in a lake
I am a flame of four colors
I am a deer standing away in the dusk
I am a field of sumac and the pomme blanche
I am an angle of geese in the winter sky
I am the hunger of a young wolf
I am the whole dream of these things
You see, I am alive, I am alive
I stand in good relation to the earth
I stand in good relation to the gods
I stand in good relation to all that is beautiful
I stand in good relation to the daughter of Tsen-tainte
You see, I am alive, I am alive

MARIANNE MOORE

Poetry

I too, dislike it: there are things that are important beyond
        all this fiddle.
  Reading it, however, with a perfect contempt for it, one discovers
        in
  it after all, a place for the genuine.
    Hands that can grasp, eyes
    that can dilate, hair that can rise
      if it must, these things are important not because a

high sounding interpretation can be put upon them but
        because they are
  useful; when they become so derivative as to become
        unintelligible,
  the same thing may be said for all of us, that we
    do not admire what
    we cannot understand: the bat
      holding on upside down or in quest of something to

eat, elephants pushing, a wild horse taking a roll, a tireless wolf under
  a tree, the immovable critic twitching his skin like a horse that
        feels a flea, the base-
  ball fan, the statistician—
    nor is it valid
      to discriminate against "business documents and

school-books"; all these phenomena are important. One must
        make a distinction
  however: when dragged into prominence by half poets, the result
        is not poetry,
  nor till the poets among us can be
    "literalists of
    the imagination"—above
      insolence and triviality and can present

for inspection, "imaginary gardens with real toads in them,"
　　　　　shall we have
　　it. In the meantime, if you demand on one hand,
　　the raw material of poetry in
　　　　all its rawness and
　　　　that which is on the other hand
　　　　　genuine, you are interested in poetry.

MARILYN NELSON

How I Discovered Poetry

It was like soul-kissing, the way the words
filled my mouth as Mrs. Purdy read from her desk.
All the other kids zoned an hour ahead to 3:15,
but Mrs. Purdy and I wandered lonely as clouds borne
by a breeze off Mount Parnassus. She must have seen
the darkest eyes in the room brim: The next day
she gave me a poem she'd chosen especially for me
to read to the all except for me white class.
She smiled when she told me to read it, smiled harder,
said oh yes I could. She smiled harder and harder
until I stood and opened my mouth to banjo playing
darkies, pickaninnies, disses and dats. When I finished
my classmates stared at the floor. We walked silent
to the buses, awed by the power of words.

The Poet

Out of the deep and the dark,
A sparkling mystery, a shape,
Something perfect,
Comes like the stir of the day:
One whose breath is an odor,
Whose eyes show the road to stars,
The breeze in his face,
The glory of heaven on his back.
He steps like a vision hung in air,
Diffusing the passion of eternity;
His abode is the sunlight of morn,
The music of eve his speech:
In his sight,
One shall turn from the dust of the grave,
And move upward to the woodland.

WILFRED OWEN

Dulce et Decorum Est

Bent double, like old beggars under sacks,
Knock-kneed, coughing like hags, we cursed through
    sludge,
Till on the haunting flares we turned our backs
And towards our distant rest began to trudge.
Men marched asleep. Many had lost their boots
But limped on, blood-shod. All went lame; all blind;
Drunk with fatigue; deaf even to the hoots
Of gas-shells dropping softly behind.

Gas! GAS! Quick, boys!—An ecstasy of fumbling,
Fitting the clumsy helmets just in time;
But someone still was yelling out and stumbling
And flound'ring like a man in fire or lime . . .
Dim, through the misty panes and thick green light,
As under a green sea, I saw him drowning.

In all my dreams, before my helpless sight,
He plunges at me, guttering, choking, drowning.

If in some smothering dreams you too could pace
Behind the wagon that we flung him in,
And watch the white eyes writhing in his face,
His hanging face, like a devil's sick of sin;
If you could hear, at every jolt, the blood
Come gargling from the froth-corrupted lungs,
Obscene as cancer, bitter as the cud
Of vile, incurable sores on innocent tongues,—
My friend, you would not tell with such high zest
To children ardent for some desperate glory,
The old Lie: Dulce et decorum est
Pro patria mori.*

---

*From the Roman poet Horace: "It is sweet and fitting to die for one's country."

DOROTHY PARKER

One Perfect Rose

A single flow'r he sent me, since we met.
    All tenderly his messenger he chose;
Deep-hearted, pure, with scented dew still wet—
    One perfect rose.

I knew the language of the floweret;
    "My fragile leaves," it said, "his heart enclose."
Love long has taken for his amulet
    One perfect rose.

Why is it no one ever sent me yet
    One perfect limousine, do you suppose?
Ah no, it's always just my luck to get
    One perfect rose.

KATHERINE PHILIPS

Epitaph

On her Son H.P. at St. Syth's Church where her body also lies interred

What on Earth deserves our trust?
Youth and Beauty both are dust.
Long we gathering are with pain,
What one moment calls again.
Seven years childless marriage past,
A Son, a son is born at last:
So exactly lim'd and fair,
Full of good Spirits, Meen, and Air,
As a long life promised,
Yet, in less than six weeks dead.
Too promising, too great a mind
In so small room to be confined:
Therefore, as fit in Heaven to dwell,
He quickly broke the Prison shell.
So the subtle Alchemist,
Can't with *Hermes* Seal resist
The powerful spirit's subtler flight,
But t'will bid him long good night.
And so the Sun if it arise
Half so glorious as his Eyes,
Like this Infant, takes a shrowd,
Buried in a morning Cloud.

EDGAR ALLAN POE

Annabel Lee

It was many and many a year ago,
    In a kingdom by the sea,
That a maiden there lived whom you may know
    By the name of Annabel Lee;
And this maiden she lived with no other thought
    Than to love and be loved by me.

I was a child and *she* was a child,
    In this kingdom by the sea,
But we loved with a love that was more than love—
    I and my Annabel Lee—
With a love that the wingèd seraphs of Heaven
    Coveted her and me.

And this was the reason that, long ago,
    In this kingdom by the sea,
A wind blew out of a cloud, chilling
    My beautiful Annabel Lee;
So that her highborn kinsmen came
    And bore her away from me,
To shut her up in a sepulchre
    In this kingdom by the sea.

The angels, not half so happy in Heaven,
    Went envying her and me—
Yes!—that was the reason (as all men know,
    In this kingdom by the sea)
That the wind came out of the cloud by night,
    Chilling and killing my Annabel Lee.

But our love it was stronger by far than the love
    Of those who were older than we—
    Of many far wiser than we—
And neither the angels in Heaven above
    Nor the demons down under the sea
Can ever dissever my soul from the soul
    Of the beautiful Annabel Lee;

For the moon never beams, without bringing me dreams
    Of the beautiful Annabel Lee;
And the stars never rise, but I feel the bright eyes
    Of the beautiful Annabel Lee;
And so, all the night-tide, I lie down by the side
    Of my darling—my darling—my life and my bride,
    In her sepulchre there by the sea—
    In her tomb by the sounding sea.

ALEXANDER POPE

Ode on Solitude

Happy the man, whose wish and care
   A few paternal acres bound,
Content to breathe his native air,
          In his own ground.

Whose herds with milk, whose fields with bread,
   Whose flocks supply him with attire,
Whose trees in summer yield him shade,
          In winter fire.

Blest, who can unconcernedly find
   Hours, days, and years slide soft away,
In health of body, peace of mind,
          Quiet by day,

Sound sleep by night; study and ease,
   Together mixed; sweet recreation;
And innocence, which most does please,
          With meditation.

Thus let me live, unseen, unknown;
   Thus unlamented let me die;
Steal from the world, and not a stone
          Tell where I lie.

EZRA POUND

Envoi

Go, dumb-born book,
Tell her that sang me once that song of Lawes:
Hadst thou but song
As thou hast subjects known,
Then were there cause in thee that should condone
Even my faults that heavy upon me lie
And build her glories their longevity.

Tell her that sheds
Such treasure in the air,
Recking naught else but that her graces give
Life to the moment,
I would bid them live
As roses might, in magic amber laid,
Red overwrought with orange and all made
One substance and one colour
Braving time.

Tell her that goes
With song upon her lips
But sings not out the song, nor knows
The maker of it, some other mouth,
May be as fair as hers,
Might, in new ages, gain her worshippers,
When our two dusts with Waller's shall be laid,
Siftings on siftings in oblivion,
Till change hath broken down
All things save Beauty alone.

SIR WALTER RALEGH

The Nymph's Reply to the Shepherd

If all the world and love were young,
And truth in every Shepherd's tongue,
These pretty pleasures might me move,
To live with thee, and be thy love.

Time drives the flocks from field to fold,
When Rivers rage and Rocks grow cold,
And *Philomel* becometh dumb,
The rest complains of cares to come.

The flowers do fade, and wanton fields,
To wayward winter reckoning yields,
A honey tongue, a heart of gall,
Is fancy's spring, but sorrow's fall.

Thy gowns, thy shoes, thy beds of Roses,
Thy cap, thy kirtle, and thy posies
Soon break, soon wither, soon forgotten:
In folly ripe, in reason rotten.

Thy belt of straw and Ivy buds,
The Coral clasps and amber studs,
All these in me no means can move
To come to thee and be thy love.

But could youth last, and love still breed,
Had joys no date, nor age no need,
Then these delights my mind might move
To live with thee, and be thy love.

DUDLEY RANDALL

Ballad of Birmingham

(On the bombing of a church in Birmingham, Alabama, 1963)

"Mother dear, may I go downtown
Instead of out to play,
And march the streets of Birmingham
In a Freedom March today?"

"No, baby, no, you may not go,
For the dogs are fierce and wild,
And clubs and hoses, guns and jails
Aren't good for a little child."

"But, mother, I won't be alone.
Other children will go with me,
And march the streets of Birmingham
To make our country free."

"No, baby, no, you may not go,
For I fear those guns will fire.
But you may go to church instead
And sing in the children's choir."

She has combed and brushed her night-dark hair,
And bathed rose petal sweet,
And drawn white gloves on her small brown hands,
And white shoes on her feet.

The mother smiled to know her child
Was in the sacred place,
But that smile was the last smile
To come upon her face.

For when she heard the explosion,
Her eyes grew wet and wild.
She raced through the streets of Birmingham
Calling for her child.

She clawed through bits of glass and brick,
Then lifted out a shoe.
"O, here's the shoe my baby wore,
But, baby, where are you?"

Miniver Cheevy

Miniver Cheevy, child of scorn,
  Grew lean while he assailed the seasons;
He wept that he was ever born,
  And he had reasons.

Miniver loved the days of old
  When swords were bright and steeds were prancing;
The vision of a warrior bold
  Would set him dancing.

Miniver sighed for what was not,
  And dreamed, and rested from his labors;
He dreamed of Thebes and Camelot,
  And Priam's neighbors.

Miniver mourned the ripe renown
  That made so many a name so fragrant;
He mourned Romance, now on the town,
  And Art, a vagrant.

Miniver loved the Medici,
  Albeit he had never seen one;
He would have sinned incessantly
  Could he have been one.

Miniver cursed the commonplace
  And eyed a khaki suit with loathing;
He missed the mediæval grace
  Of iron clothing.

Miniver scorned the gold he sought,
  But sore annoyed was he without it;
Miniver thought, and thought, and thought,
  And thought about it.

Miniver Cheevy, born too late,
  Scratched his head and kept on thinking;
Miniver coughed, and called it fate,
  And kept on drinking.

CHRISTINA ROSSETTI

Up-Hill

Does the road wind up-hill all the way?
    Yes, to the very end.
Will the day's journey take the whole long day?
    From morn to night, my friend.

But is there for the night a resting-place?
    A roof for when the slow dark hours begin.
May not the darkness hide it from my face?
    You cannot miss that inn.

Shall I meet other wayfarers at night?
    Those who have gone before.
Then must I knock, or call when just in sight?
    They will not keep you standing at that door.

Shall I find comfort, travel-sore and weak?
    Of labour you shall find the sum.
Will there be beds for me and all who seek?
    Yea, beds for all who come.

BENJAMIN ALIRE SÁENZ

To the Desert

I came to you one rainless August night.
You taught me how to live without the rain.
You are thirst and thirst is all I know.
You are sand, wind, sun, and burning sky,
The hottest blue. You blow a breeze and brand
Your breath into my mouth. You reach—then *bend*
Your force, to break, blow, burn, and make me new.
You wrap your name tight around my ribs
And keep me warm. I was born for you.
Above, below, by you, by you surrounded.
I wake to you at dawn. Never break your
Knot. Reach, rise, blow, *Sálvame, mi dios,*
Trágame, mi tierra. Salva, traga, Break me,
I am bread. I will be the water for your thirst.

CARL SANDBURG

Chicago

Hog Butcher for the World,
Tool Maker, Stacker of Wheat,
Player with Railroads and the Nation's Freight Handler;
Stormy, husky, brawling,
City of the Big Shoulders:

They tell me you are wicked and I believe them, for I
      have seen your painted women under the gas lamps
      luring the farm boys.
And they tell me you are crooked and I answer: Yes, it
      is true I have seen the gunman kill and go free to
      kill again.
And they tell me you are brutal and my reply is: On the
      faces of women and children I have seen the marks
      of wanton hunger.
And having answered so I turn once more to those who
      sneer at this my city, and I give them back the sneer
      and say to them:
Come and show me another city with lifted head singing
      so proud to be alive and coarse and strong and cunning.
Flinging magnetic curses amid the toil of piling job on
      job, here is a tall bold slugger set vivid against the
      little soft cities;
Fierce as a dog with tongue lapping for action, cunning
      as a savage pitted against the wilderness,
              Bareheaded,
              Shoveling,
              Wrecking,
              Planning,
              Building, breaking, rebuilding,
Under the smoke, dust all over his mouth, laughing with
      white teeth,

Under the terrible burden of destiny laughing as a young
    man laughs,
Laughing even as an ignorant fighter laughs who has
    never lost a battle,
Bragging and laughing that under his wrist is the pulse,
    and under his ribs the heart of the people,
                    Laughing!
Laughing the stormy, husky, brawling laughter of
    Youth, half-naked, sweating, proud to be Hog
    Butcher, Tool Maker, Stacker of Wheat, Player with
    Railroads and Freight Handler to the Nation.

WILLIAM SHAKESPEARE

When, in disgrace with fortune and men's eyes (29)

When, in disgrace with fortune and men's eyes,
I all alone beweep my outcast state,
And trouble deaf heaven with my bootless cries,
And look upon myself and curse my fate,
Wishing me like to one more rich in hope,
Featured like him, like him with friends possessed,
Desiring this man's art and that man's scope,
With what I most enjoy contented least;
Yet in these thoughts myself almost despising,
Haply I think on thee, and then my state,
(Like to the lark at break of day arising
From sullen earth) sings hymns at heaven's gate;
    For thy sweet love remembered such wealth brings
    That then I scorn to change my state with kings.

Not marble, nor the gilded monuments (55)

Not marble, nor the gilded monuments
Of princes, shall outlive this powerful rhyme
But you shall shine more bright in these contents
Than unswept stone, besmeared with sluttish time.
When wasteful war shall statues overturn,
And broils root out the work of masonry,
Nor Mars his sword nor war's quick fire shall burn
The living record of your memory.
'Gainst death and all-oblivious enmity
Shall you pace forth; your praise shall still find room
Even in the eyes of all posterity
That wear this world out to the ending doom.
 So, till the Judgement that yourself arise,
 You live in this, and dwell in lovers' eyes.

PERCY BYSSHE SHELLEY

Ozymandias

I met a traveller from an antique land,
Who said: "Two vast and trunkless legs of stone
Stand in the desert. Near them, on the sand,
Half sunk, a shattered visage lies, whose frown,
And wrinkled lip, and sneer of cold command,
Tell that its sculptor well those passions read
Which yet survive, stamped on these lifeless things,
The hand that mocked them and the heart that fed;
And on the pedestal these words appear:
"My name is Ozymandias, king of kings;
Look on my works, ye mighty, and despair!"
Nothing beside remains. Round the decay
Of that colossal wreck, boundless and bare
The lone and level sands stretch far away.

CHARLOTTE SMITH

Oh, Hope! thou soother sweet of human woes

Oh, Hope! thou soother sweet of human woes!
  How shall I lure thee to my haunts forlorn!
For me wilt thou renew the withered rose,
  And clear my painful path of pointed thorn?
Ah come, sweet nymph! in smiles and softness drest,
  Like the young hours that lead the tender year
Enchantress come! and charm my cares to rest:
  Alas! the flatterer flies, and will not hear!
A prey to fear, anxiety, and pain,
  Must I a sad existence still deplore?
Lo! the flowers fade, but all the thorns remain,
  'For me the vernal garland blooms no more.'
Come then, 'pale Misery's love!' be thou my cure,
And I will bless thee, who though slow art sure.

WALLACE STEVENS

Thirteen Ways of Looking at a Blackbird

I

Among twenty snowy mountains,
The only moving thing
Was the eye of the blackbird.

II

I was of three minds,
Like a tree
In which there are three blackbirds.

III

The blackbird whirled in the autumn winds.
It was a small part of the pantomime.

IV

A man and a woman
Are one.
A man and a woman and a blackbird
Are one.

V

I do not know which to prefer,
The beauty of inflections
Or the beauty of innuendoes,
The blackbird whistling
Or just after.

VI

Icicles filled the long window
With barbaric glass.
The shadow of the blackbird
Crossed it, to and fro.
The mood
Traced in the shadow
An indecipherable cause.

VII

O thin men of Haddam,
Why do you imagine golden birds?
Do you not see how the blackbird
Walks around the feet
Of the women about you?

VIII

I know noble accents
And lucid, inescapable rhythms;
But I know, too,
That the blackbird is involved
In what I know.

IX

When the blackbird flew out of sight,
It marked the edge
Of one of many circles.

At the sight of blackbirds
Flying in a green light,
Even the bawds of euphony
Would cry out sharply.

XI

He rode over Connecticut
In a glass coach.
Once, a fear pierced him,
In that he mistook
The shadow of his equipage
For blackbirds.

XII

The river is moving.
The blackbird must be flying.

XIII

It was evening all afternoon.
It was snowing
And it was going to snow.
The blackbird sat
In the cedar-limbs.

JONATHAN SWIFT

A Satirical Elegy on the Death of a Late Famous General

His Grace! impossible! what dead!
Of old age too, and in his bed!
And could that mighty warrior fall?
And so inglorious, after all!
Well, since he's gone, no matter how,
The last loud trump must wake him now:
And, trust me, as the noise grows stronger,
He'd wish to sleep a little longer.
And could he be indeed so old
As by the newspapers we're told?
Threescore, I think, is pretty high;
'Twas time in conscience he should die
This world he cumbered long enough;
He burnt his candle to the snuff;
And that's the reason, some folks think,
He left behind so great a stink.
Behold his funeral appears,
Nor widow's sighs, nor orphan's tears,
Wont at such times each heart to pierce,
Attend the progress of his hearse.
But what of that, his friends may say,
He had those honours in his day.
True to his profit and his pride,
He made them weep before he died.

Come hither, all ye empty things,
Ye bubbles raised by breath of kings;
Who float upon the tide of state,
Come hither, and behold your fate.
Let pride be taught by this rebuke,
How very mean a thing's a Duke;
From all his ill-got honours flung,
Turned to that dirt from whence he sprung.

RABINDRANATH TAGORE

Gitanjali 35

Where the mind is without fear and the head is held high;
　　Where knowledge is free;
　　Where the world has not been broken up into fragments by
　　　　narrow domestic walls;
　　Where words come out from the depth of truth;
　　Where tireless striving stretches its arms towards perfection;
　　Where the clear stream of reason has not lost its way into the
　　　　dreary desert sand of dead habit;
　　Where the mind is led forward by thee into ever-widening
　　　　thought and action—
　　Into that heaven of freedom, my Father, let my country awake.

SARA TEASDALE

Let It Be Forgotten

Let it be forgotten, as a flower is forgotten,
    Forgotten as a fire that once was singing gold,
Let it be forgotten for ever and ever,
    Time is a kind friend, he will make us old.

If anyone asks, say it was forgotten
    Long and long ago,
As a flower, as a fire, as a hushed footfall
    In a long forgotten snow.

ALFRED, LORD TENNYSON

The Charge of the Light Brigade

I

Half a league, half a league,
Half a league onward,
All in the valley of Death
    Rode the six hundred.
"Forward, the Light Brigade!
Charge for the guns!" he said.
Into the valley of Death
    Rode the six hundred.

II

"Forward, the Light Brigade!"
Was there a man dismayed?
Not though the soldier knew
    Someone had blundered.
    Theirs not to make reply,
    Theirs not to reason why,
    Theirs but to do and die.
    Into the valley of Death
    Rode the six hundred.

III

Cannon to right of them,
Cannon to left of them,
Cannon in front of them
    Volleyed and thundered;
Stormed at with shot and shell,
Boldly they rode and well,
Into the jaws of Death,
Into the mouth of hell
    Rode the six hundred.

IV

Flashed all their sabres bare,
Flashed as they turned in air
Sab'ring the gunners there,
Charging an army, while
    All the world wondered.
Plunged in the battery-smoke
Right thro' the line they broke;
Cossack and Russian
Reeled from the sabre stroke
    Shattered and sundered.
Then they rode back, but not
    Not the six hundred.

V

Cannon to right of them,
Cannon to left of them,
Cannon behind them
    Volleyed and thundered;
Stormed at with shot and shell,
While horse and hero fell.
They that had fought so well
Came through the jaws of Death,
Back from the mouth of hell,
All that was left of them,
    Left of six hundred.

VI

When can their glory fade?
O the wild charge they made!
    All the world wondered.
Honour the charge they made!
Honour the Light Brigade,
    Noble six hundred!

DYLAN THOMAS

Do Not Go Gentle into That Good Night

Do not go gentle into that good night,
Old age should burn and rave at close of day;
Rage, rage against the dying of the light.

Though wise men at their end know dark is right,
Because their words had forked no lightning they
Do not go gentle into that good night.

Good men, the last wave by, crying how bright
Their frail deeds might have danced in a green bay,
Rage, rage against the dying of the light.

Wild men who caught and sang the sun in flight,
And learn, too late, they grieved it on its way,
Do not go gentle into that good night.

Grave men, near death, who see with blinding sight
Blind eyes could blaze like meteors and be gay,
Rage, rage against the dying of the light.

And you, my father, there on the sad height,
Curse, bless, me now with your fierce tears, I pray,
Do not go gentle into that good night.
Rage, rage against the dying of the light.

Fern Hill

Now as I was young and easy under the apple boughs
About the lilting house and happy as the grass was green,
  The night above the dingle starry,
    Time let me hail and climb
  Golden in the heydays of his eyes,
And honoured among wagons I was prince of the apple towns
And once below a time I lordly had the trees and leaves
    Trail with daisies and barley
  Down the rivers of the windfall light.

And as I was green and carefree, famous among the barns
About the happy yard and singing as the farm was home,
  In the sun that is young once only,
    Time let me play and be
  Golden in the mercy of his means,
And green and golden I was huntsman and herdsman, the calves
Sang to my horn, the foxes on the hills barked clear and cold,
    And the sabbath rang slowly
  In the pebbles of the holy streams.

All the sun long it was running, it was lovely, the hay
Fields high as the house, the tunes from the chimneys, it was air
  And playing, lovely and watery
    And fire green as grass.
  And nightly under the simple stars
As I rode to sleep the owls were bearing the farm away,
All the moon long I heard, blessed among stables, the nightjars
    Flying with the ricks, and the horses
      Flashing into the dark.

And then to awake, and the farm, like a wanderer white
With the dew, come back, the cock on his shoulder: it was all
    Shining, it was Adam and maiden,
        The sky gathered again
    And the sun grew round that very day.
So it must have been after the birth of the simple light
In the first, spinning place, the spellbound horses walking warm
    Out of the whinnying green stable
        On to the fields of praise.

And honoured among foxes and pheasants by the gay house
Under the new made clouds and happy as the heart was long,
    In the sun born over and over,
        I ran my heedless ways,
    My wishes raced through the house high hay
And nothing I cared, at my sky blue trades, that time allows
In all his tuneful turning so few and such morning songs
    Before the children green and golden
        Follow him out of grace,

Nothing I cared, in the lamb white days, that time would take me
Up to the swallow thronged loft by the shadow of my hand,
    In the moon that is always rising,
        Nor that riding to sleep
    I should hear him fly with the high fields
And wake to the farm forever fled from the childless land.
Oh as I was young and easy in the mercy of his means,
    Time held me green and dying
    Though I sang in my chains like the sea.

JEAN TOOMER

November Cotton Flower

Boll-weevil's coming, and the winter's cold,
Made cotton-stalks look rusty, season's old,
And cotton, scarce as any southern snow,
Was vanishing; the branch, so pinched and slow,
Failed in its function as the autumn rake;
Drouth fighting soil had caused the soil to take
All water from the streams; dead birds were found
In wells a hundred feet below the ground—
Such was the season when the flower bloomed.
Old folks were startled, and it soon assumed
Significance. Superstition saw
Something it had never seen before:
Brown eyes that loved without a trace of fear,
Beauty so sudden for that time of year.

AMY UYEMATSU

Deliberate

So by sixteen we move in packs
learn to strut and slide
in deliberate lowdown rhythm
talk in a syn/co/pa/ted beat
because we want so bad
to be cool, never to be mistaken
for white, even when we leave
these rowdier L.A. streets—
remember how we paint our eyes
like gangsters
flash our legs in nylons
sassy black high heels
or two inch zippered boots
stack them by the door at night
next to Daddy's muddy gardening shoes.

EDMUND WALLER

Song

Go, lovely rose!
Tell her that wastes her time and me,
That now she knows,
When I resemble her to thee,
How sweet and fair she seems to be.

Tell her that's young,
And shuns to have her graces spied,
That hadst thou sprung
In deserts, where no men abide,
Thou must have uncommended died.

Small is the worth
Of beauty from the light retired;
Bid her come forth,
Suffer herself to be desired,
And not blush so to be admired.

Then die! that she
The common fate of all things rare
May read in thee;
How small a part of time they share
That are so wondrous sweet and fair!

PHILLIS WHEATLEY

On Virtue

O thou bright jewel in my aim I strive
To comprehend thee. Thine own words declare
Wisdom is higher than a fool can reach.
I cease to wonder, and no more attempt
Thine height t'explore, or fathom thy profound.
But, O my soul, sink not into despair,
Virtue is near thee, and with gentle hand
Would now embrace thee, hovers o'er thine head.
Fain would the heaven-born soul with her converse,
Then seek, then court her for her promised bliss.

Auspicious queen, thine heavenly pinions spread,
And lead celestial *Chastity* along;
Lo! now her sacred retinue descends,
Arrayed in glory from the orbs above.
Attend me, *Virtue*, thro' my youthful years!
O leave me not to the false joys of time!
But guide my steps to endless life and bliss.
Greatness, or *Goodness*, say what I shall call thee,
To give an higher appellation still,
Teach me a better strain, a nobler lay,
O Thou, enthroned with Cherubs in the realms of day!

WALT WHITMAN

I Hear America Singing

I hear America singing, the varied carols I hear,
Those of mechanics, each one singing his as it should be blithe and
    strong,
The carpenter singing his as he measures his plank or beam,
The mason singing his as he makes ready for work, or leaves off work,
The boatman singing what belongs to him in his boat, the deckhand
    singing on the steamboat deck,
The shoemaker singing as he sits on his bench, the hatter singing as he
    stands,
The wood-cutter's song, the ploughboy's on his way in the morning,
    or at noon intermission or at sundown,
The delicious singing of the mother, or of the young wife at work, or
    of the girl sewing or washing,
Each singing what belongs to him or her and to none else,
The day what belongs to the day—at night the party of young
    fellows, robust, friendly,
Singing with open mouths their strong melodious songs.

JOHN GREENLEAF WHITTIER

Barbara Frietchie

Up from the meadows rich with corn,
Clear in the cool September morn,

The clustered spires of Frederick stand
Green-walled by the hills of Maryland.

Round about them orchards sweep,
Apple- and peach-tree fruited deep,

Fair as a garden of the Lord
To the eyes of the famished rebel horde,

On that pleasant morn of the early fall
When Lee marched over the mountain wall,—

Over the mountains winding down,
Horse and foot, into Frederick town.

Forty flags with their silver stars,
Forty flags with their crimson bars,

Flapped in the morning wind: the sun
Of noon looked down, and saw not one.

Up rose old Barbara Frietchie then,
Bowed with her fourscore years and ten;

Bravest of all in Frederick town,
She took up the flag the men hauled down;

In her attic window the staff she set,
To show that one heart was loyal yet.

Up the street came the rebel tread,
Stonewall Jackson riding ahead.

Under his slouched hat left and right
He glanced: the old flag met his sight.

"Halt!"— the dust-brown ranks stood fast.
"Fire!"— out blazed the rifle-blast.

It shivered the window, pane and sash;
It rent the banner with seam and gash.

Quick, as it fell, from the broken staff
Dame Barbara snatched the silken scarf;

She leaned far out on the window-sill,
And shook it forth with a royal will.

"Shoot, if you must, this old gray head,
But spare your country's flag," she said.

A shade of sadness, a blush of shame,
Over the face of the leader came;

The nobler nature within him stirred
To life at that woman's deed and word:

"Who touches a hair of yon gray head
Dies like a dog! March on!" he said.

All day long through Frederick street
Sounded the tread of marching feet:

All day long that free flag tost
Over the heads of the rebel host.

Ever its torn folds rose and fell
On the loyal winds that loved it well;

And through the hill-gaps sunset light
Shone over it with a warm good-night.

Barbara Frietchie's work is o'er,
And the Rebel rides on his raids no more.

Honor to her! and let a tear
Fall, for her sake, on Stonewall's bier.

Over Barbara Frietchie's grave
Flag of Freedom and Union, wave!

Peace and order and beauty draw
Round thy symbol of light and law;

And ever the stars above look down
On thy stars below in Frederick town!

WILLIAM CARLOS WILLIAMS

Danse Russe

If when my wife is sleeping
and the baby and Kathleen
are sleeping
and the sun is a flame-white disc
in silken mists
above shining trees,—
if I in my north room
dance naked, grotesquely
before my mirror
waving my shirt round my head
and singing softly to myself:
"I am lonely, lonely.
I was born to be lonely,
I am best so!"
If I admire my arms, my face,
my shoulders, flanks, buttocks
against the yellow drawn shades,—

Who shall say I am not
the happy genius of my household?

WILLIAM WORDSWORTH

The World Is Too Much with Us

The world is too much with us; late and soon,
Getting and spending, we lay waste our powers;—
Little we see in Nature that is ours;
We have given our hearts away, a sordid boon!
This Sea that bares her bosom to the moon;
The winds that will be howling at all hours,
And are up-gathered now like sleeping flowers;
For this, for everything, we are out of tune;
It moves us not. Great God! I'd rather be
A Pagan suckled in a creed outworn;
So might I, standing on this pleasant lea,
Have glimpses that would make me less forlorn;
Have sight of Proteus rising from the sea;
Or hear old Triton blow his wreathèd horn.

SIR THOMAS WYATT

They flee from me that sometime did me seek

They flee from me that sometime did me seek
With naked foot, stalking in my chamber.
I have seen them gentle, tame, and meek,
That now are wild and do not remember
That sometime they put themself in danger
To take bread at my hand; and now they range,
Busily seeking with a continual change.

Thanked be fortune it hath been otherwise
Twenty times better; but once in special,
In thin array after a pleasant guise,
When her loose gown from her shoulders did fall,
And she me caught in her arms long and small;
Therewithall sweetly did me kiss
And softly said, "Dear heart, how like you this?"

It was no dream: I lay broad waking.
But all is turned thorough my gentleness
Into a strange fashion of forsaking;
And I have leave to go of her goodness,
And she also, to use newfangleness.
But since that I so kindly am served
I would fain know what she hath deserved.

ELINOR WYLIE

Cold Blooded Creatures

Man, the egregious egoist,
(In mystery the twig is bent,)
Imagines, by some mental twist,
That he alone is sentient

Of the intolerable load
Which on all living creatures lies,
Nor stoops to pity in the toad
The speechless sorrow of its eyes.

He asks no questions of the snake,
Nor plumbs the phosphorescent gloom
Where lidless fishes, broad awake,
Swim staring at a night-mare doom.

WILLIAM BUTLER YEATS

The Lake Isle of Innisfree

I will arise and go now, and go to Innisfree,
And a small cabin build there, of clay and wattles made;
Nine bean-rows will I have there, a hive for the honey-bee,
And live alone in the bee-loud glade.

And I shall have some peace there, for peace comes dropping slow,
Dropping from the veils of the morning to where the cricket sings;
There midnight's all a glimmer, and noon a purple glow,
And evening full of the linnet's wings.

I will arise and go now, for always night and day
I hear lake water lapping with low sounds by the shore;
While I stand on the roadway, or on the pavements grey,
I hear it in the deep heart's core.

When You Are Old

When you are old and grey and full of sleep,
And nodding by the fire, take down this book,
And slowly read, and dream of the soft look
Your eyes had once, and of their shadows deep;

How many loved your moments of glad grace,
And loved your beauty with love false or true,
But one man loved the pilgrim soul in you,
And loved the sorrows of your changing face;

And bending down beside the glowing bars,
Murmur, a little sadly, how Love fled
And paced upon the mountains overhead
And hid his face amid a crowd of stars.

NOTES & CREDITS

BIOGRAPHICAL NOTES

MATTHEW ARNOLD (1822 – 1888), poet and essayist, sharply criticized the materialism of the Victorians. "Dover Beach" anticipates twentieth-century modernist poets in contemplating a world where old beliefs and values have withered. In his influential *Culture and Anarchy*, he argues that culture could unify society by making "the best that has been thought and known in the world current everywhere."

W(YSTAN) H(UGH) AUDEN (1907 – 1973) grew up in Birmingham, England and was known for his extraordinary intellect and wit. His first book, *Poems*, was published in 1930 with the help of T.S. Eliot. Just before World War II broke out, Auden emigrated to the United States where he met the poet Chester Kallman who became his lifelong lover. Auden won the Pulitzer Prize in 1948 for *The Age of Anxiety*.

APHRA BEHN (1640 – 1689) was the first English woman to earn her living as a writer. Her fiction — including a work critical of slavery — is often political and her plays are frequently bawdy. She sometimes scandalized her audience, but her work broke new literary ground and sold well.

AMBROSE BIERCE (1842 – 1914?) was a journalist, short story writer, poet, and satirist who wrote about the culture around him with fearlessness and wit. He was one of the most popular writers of his time, and his book *The Devil's Dictionary*, a collection of skewering aphorisms, remains a classic. Bierce disappeared mysteriously after deciding to go to war-torn Mexico at the age of seventy-one.

WILLIAM BLAKE (1757 – 1827) was born in London, where he spent most of his life working as an engraver and illustrator. At about age ten, Blake had his first vision: a tree filled with angels. Mysticism is one of the hallmarks of his work. While his poetry was not widely known during his lifetime, his writing and his art have continued to grow in popularity.

LOUISE BOGAN (1897 – 1970) published most of her poetry before age 40. Her first collection, *Body of this Death*, appeared in 1923 and her sixth, *The Sleeping Fury*, in 1937. Her work is often exactingly formal yet intensely personal. She reviewed poetry for the *New Yorker* for 38 years, becoming one of America's most astute critics.

ANNE BRADSTREET (1612 – 1672) is generally considered the first American poet. Born around 1612 near Northampton, England, she married Simon Bradstreet at age 16, and the couple emigrated to the New World in 1630. In such bestselling collections as *The Tenth Muse Lately Sprung Up in America*, Bradstreet wrote of her life as a mother, wife, and daughter during the establishment of the Massachusetts Bay Colony.

EMILY BRONTË's (1818 – 1848) first verses appeared in a book with work by her sisters Charlotte and Anne, pseudonymously titled *Poems by Currer, Ellis, and Acton Bell* in order to conceal the authors' gender. Emily's poems are distinguished from her siblings' by their sober tone and visionary spirituality, qualities also found in her famous novel, *Wuthering Heights*.

When RUPERT BROOKE (1887 – 1915) died at the age of 27, he was immortalized as a charismatic poet whom W.B. Yeats called "the handsomest young man in England," and as a symbol of what would be known as the "Lost Generation." His patriotic poetry strengthened support for World War I, although he did not see much combat.

GWENDOLYN BROOKS (1917 – 2000) was born in Topeka, Kansas, though she spent most of her life on Chicago's south side, whose Bronzeville neighborhood she memorialized in her poetry. She received the Pulitzer Prize — the first African American so honored — for *Annie Allen* in 1950. One of her best-loved poems, "we real cool," is about the short, sad lives of pool-playing truants. Brooks was devoted to encouraging young people to write.

ELIZABETH BARRETT BROWNING (1806 – 1861) began writing as a young girl in Durham, England. Despite a nervous collapse, a period of grief occasioned by the untimely deaths of two brothers, and a lifetime of illness, she continued to write poetry and essays about politics and social injustices, eventually becoming one of the greatest writers of the Victorian Era. In 1846 she eloped to Florence, Italy, with Robert Browning, to whom she dedicated her best-known book, *Sonnets from the Portuguese*.

ROBERT BROWNING (1812–1889) was born in Camberwell, England, and his education mostly took place among his father's 6,000-book library. As a writer, Browning was regarded as a failure for many years, living in the shadow of his wife Elizabeth Barrett Browning. However, late in life Browning's brilliant use of dramatic monologue made him a literary icon. Today, his most widely read work is *Men and Women*, a collection of dramatic monologues dedicated to his wife.

ROBERT BURNS (1759–1796) is considered the unofficial national poet of Scotland. He wrote some poetry in standard English, but his poems and songs in Scottish dialect are better remembered. His patriotic poem "Scots Wha Hae" stirs Scottish sentiment to this day, and his song "Auld Lang Syne" is synonymous with New Year's Eve.

GEORGE GORDON, LORD BYRON'S (1788–1824) adventurous life overshadows his work: he became a British peer at age ten, traveled widely, was cast out of society for scandalous love affairs, and died while preparing for battle. However, his Romantic poetry has inspired writers, composers, moody loners, and rebels around the world. Artists as diverse as French composer Hector Berlioz and Russian poet Alexander Pushkin have cited his work as a major influence.

THOMAS CAMPION (1567–1620), born in London, practiced medicine to support himself, but his passions were poetry and music. Especially fond of epigrams, he published *Epigrammatum Libri II*, a collection of 453 of the short poems. Campion also published several books of ayres, which are non-religious songs for a solo voice, and even wrote libretti for masques performed in King James's court.

Since *Alice's Adventures in Wonderland* first appeared in 1865, LEWIS CARROLL'S (Charles Lutwidge Dodgson, 1832–1898) works have been loved by children and adults alike. His nonsense poetry and invented language create clear images of fantastic landscapes, animals, and heroes.

LADY MARY CHUDLEIGH (1656–1710) was a devout Anglican who educated herself and, ahead of her time, challenged traditional gender roles. "To the Ladies" appeared in *Poems on Several Occasions* (1703);

it echoes the feminist argument she set forth in *The Female Advocate; or, A Plea for the Just Liberty of the Tender Sex and Particularly of Married Women.*

JOHN CLARE (1793–1864) was born into a peasant family in Helpston, England. Although he was the son of illiterate parents, Clare received some formal schooling. While earning money through such manual labor as ploughing and threshing, he published several volumes of poetry, including *Poems Descriptive of Rural Life and Scenery.* After suffering from delusions, Clare was admitted to an insane asylum where he spent the final 20 years of his life.

LUCILLE CLIFTON (b. 1936) was born in Depew, New York, and educated at Howard University, where she met fellow writers Sterling Brown, A.B. Spellman, and Toni Morrison. Clifton's free verse lyrics — spare in form — often concern the importance of family and community in the face of economic oppression. Though rooted in folktales and a strong tradition of storytelling, many of Clifton's poems are spirited, sometimes spiritual, explorations of race and gender.

SAMUEL TAYLOR COLERIDGE (1772–1834) published *The Lyrical Ballads* with William Wordsworth in 1798, an event later seen as the beginning of the Romantic movement in England. Coleridge held imagination to be the vital force behind poetry, and distinguished among different kinds of imagination in his long prose work *Biographia Literaria.* The haunting imagery of his poems "The Rime of the Ancient Mariner" and "Kubla Khan" is familiar to millions of readers.

Born in Garrettsville, Ohio, HART CRANE (1899–1932) left his unhappy home for New York before his last year of high school. He planned — against his father's wishes — to pursue a career as a poet. Crane became part of the poetry scene in Greenwich Village where he produced his most important work, the book-length poem *The Bridge.* At age 33 Crane committed suicide by jumping from the deck of a steamship en route from Mexico to New York.

An orphan in New York City, COUNTEE CULLEN (1903–1946) was adopted by a reverend and raised in a Methodist parsonage. A brilliant student, he began writing poetry at age 14 and as a student at New York University wrote most of the poems in his first three books: *Color, Copper Sun,* and *The Ballad of the Brown Girl.* Cullen became a prominent poet of the Harlem Renaissance, although some of his peers criticized him for avoiding political and social issues.

E(DWARD) E(STLIN) CUMMINGS (1894–1962) claimed to have composed a poem a day for fourteen years. Cummings developed a unique style of writing, full of experimentation with form, spelling, syntax, and punctuation. Also a painter, he called himself "an author of pictures, a draughtsman of words." Cummings's novel *The Enormous Room* describes his time spent in a World War I prison camp.

Born in Michigan, TOI DERRICOTTE (b. 1941) is the co-founder of the African-American writers retreat, Cave Canem, and Professor of English at the University of Pittsburgh. A two-time poetry fellowship recipient from the National Endowment for the Arts, her literary memoir, *The Black Notebooks*, won the 1998 Annisfield-Wolf Book Award for Nonfiction.

The famous hermit from Amherst, Massachusetts, EMILY DICKINSON (1830–1886) published only eight poems during her lifetime. Today her nearly 2,000 succinct, profound meditations on life and death, nature, love, and art make her one of the most original and important poets in English.

There are two JOHN DONNES (1572–1631): the brilliant, pleasure-seeking man-about-town who in his youth wrote frank love poems to various women along with satires that jeered his fellow men, and the sober, serious Dean of St. Paul's, an Anglican reverend famed for his moving sermons and profound "Holy Sonnets." One of the Metaphysical poets (John Dryden coined the term half a century later), Donne was known for his razor wit and his extended comparisons, also called conceits.

In a career that spanned five decades, H.D. (Hilda Doolittle, 1886–1961) was given many labels: Imagist, feminist, mythologist, and mystic. Her abiding concern, though, was to explore and represent her personal experience as a poet and a woman. In addition to poetry, she published novels, short stories, and two epic poems on war: *Trilogy* and *Helen in Egypt*.

The first African-American woman to be named Poet Laureate of the United States, and only the second to win a Pulitzer Prize for poetry (*Thomas and Beulah*, 1987), RITA DOVE (b. 1952) has achieved a great deal in a career not yet three-decades old. Her multi-layered poems dramatize the stories of individuals both living and dead against the backdrop of larger historical forces.

The son of former slaves, PAUL LAURENCE DUNBAR (1872–1906) was the first African-American poet to reach a wide audience, publishing prolifically before his early death. His use of both dialect and standard English to portray his culture's folkways, joys, and travails distinguishes him from other writers of the time. He also spoke out against racism and injustice in essays that appeared in the *Atlantic Monthly*, the *Saturday Evening Post*, and other mainstream publications.

Arguably the most famous poet of the Modernist movement, T(HOMAS) S(TEARNS) ELIOT (1888–1965) revolutionized the art first with "The Love Song of J. Alfred Prufrock" in 1915 and then with the 1922 publication of his long, difficult poem *The Waste Land*. He also became famous for his criticism and later for the poems adapted into the Broadway musical *Cats*. Although born in St. Louis, he spent most of his adult life in England, working first in banking, then in publishing.

The daughter of Henry VIII and Anne Boleyn, QUEEN ELIZABETH I (1533–1603) ascended to the throne in 1558. Elizabeth's artful use of ambiguity infuses her writing. She produced the first English translation of Horace's *Art of Poetry*. Her respect for learning created an atmosphere conducive to the arts and education, and cultural life flourished during her reign. Edmund Spenser wrote his powerful *Faerie Queen* in her honor.

Born in Boston, RALPH WALDO EMERSON (1803–1882) followed in his father's footsteps when he became a Unitarian minister. However, after his young wife died of tuberculosis in 1831, he found his faith shaken. The next year he traveled Europe where he formed the basis of his Transcendentalist philosophy — the intuitive belief in the oneness of the world rather than in scientific rationalism or formal religion. After returning to New England, Emerson published "Nature," "Self-Reliance," and "Experience," the essays that established him as one of the most important thinkers in America.

RHINA P. ESPAILLAT (b. 1932) was born in the Dominican Republic under the dictatorship of Rafael Trujillo. After Espaillat's father opposed the regime, her family was exiled to the United States, where they settled in New York City. She began writing poetry as a young girl, first in Spanish, then English, and has published in both languages.

ANNE FINCH, COUNTESS OF WINCHILSEA (1661–1720) was well educated for a woman of her time. She had the privilege of living in the court of Charles II by serving as a maid of honor to Mary of Modena. During this time Finch secretly wrote poetry and published anonymously. *Miscellany Poems on Several Occasions* appeared in 1713, the first publication that publicly acknowledged her authorship. In 1712 her husband unexpectedly inherited the title of Earl, making Finch the Countess of Winchilsea.

ROBERT FROST (1874–1963) is considered the bard of New England. Casual readers sometimes overlook the depth of his poetry and its technical accomplishment. His apparently simple poems — collected in volumes from *A Boy's Will* to *In the Clearing* — reveal a darker heart upon close reading, and his easy conversational style is propelled by an unfaltering meter and an assiduous sensitivity to the sounds of language.

THOMAS GRAY (1716–1771) was born in London and was the only of twelve siblings to survive. Although his family had a modest income, Gray was able to attend Eton and Cambridge with his uncle's help. In 1742 he wrote his first important poems, including "Ode on a Distant Prospect of Eton College." When he wrote, he perfected each line before moving on to the next; he took years to complete "Elegy Written in a Country Churchyard," now one of the most frequently quoted English poems.

THOMAS HARDY (1840–1928) was born in Dorset County, England, where he studied architecture, but he later quit to pursue a literary career. In order to gain financial stability, Hardy first published novels, including such classics as *Tess of the D'Urbervilles* and *Jude the Obscure*. Once he was well known and well off financially, he returned to poetry, his first love. Hardy's dark, bleak verse was at odds with his Victorian contemporaries who tended to present more optimistic perspectives on life.

Like other Native-American poets such as N. Scott Momaday, Simon Ortiz, and Leslie Marmon Silko, JOY HARJO (b. 1951) writes in an effort to re-establish lost connections: with the sacred land, powerful ancestors, and fellow searchers along the margins of contemporary life. She also plays in a band called Poetic Justice.

Deeply influenced by the blues and jazz, MICHAEL S. HARPER (b. 1938) draws attention in his work to the many injustices suffered by African Americans over the course of this country's history. Then, like the musicians he so admires, out of this painful and even tragic legacy, he makes song.

Born Asa Bundy Sheffey into a poor family, ROBERT HAYDEN's (1913 – 1980) parents left him to be raised by foster parents. Due to extreme nearsightedness, Hayden turned to books rather than sports in his childhood. Some of his best-known poems can be found in his collection *A Ballad of Remembrance*. Hayden was the first African American to be appointed as Consultant in Poetry to the Library of Congress.

While GEORGE HERBERT's (1593 – 1633) early adult life centered around the secular world of the university, his later dedication to Christianity and to poetry have had a lasting effect on literature. His mother was well acquainted with John Donne, with whose work Herbert's is often associated. Herbert's poetry, although often formally experimental, is always passionate, searching, and elegant.

ROBERT HERRICK (1591 – 1674) was born in London and may have attended the Westminster School. At age 16, he was apprenticed to his uncle, a goldsmith, but he terminated the apprenticeship after six years and went to St. John's College, Cambridge, where he received a master's degree. He greatly admired Ben Jonson and became part of the group known as the "Tribe of Ben." Herrick never married; many of the women he addresses in the poem in his volume *Hesperides* may have been fictional.

OLIVER WENDELL HOLMES (1809 – 1894), born in Cambridge, Massachusetts, was a brilliant doctor who was well known for his witty lectures at Harvard. Also a poet and essayist, Holmes's prose series "The Autocrat of the Breakfast Table" first appeared in the *Atlantic Monthly* with its inaugural issue in 1857. A year later it was published as a book, which also included some of his most memorable poetry.

GERARD MANLEY HOPKINS's (1844 – 1889) family encouraged his artistic talents when he was a youth in Essex, England. However, Hopkins became estranged from his Protestant family when he converted to Roman Catholicism. Upon deciding to become a priest, he burned all of his poems and did not write again for many years. His work was not published until 30 years after his death when his friend Robert Bridges edited the volume *Poems*.

Born in Worcestershire, England, A(LFRED) E(DWARD) HOUSMAN (1859–1936) was profoundly affected by his mother's death when he was 12. Housman lived mostly as a recluse. He was a brilliant classicist, first appointed Professor of Latin at University College, London, then Trinity College, Cambridge. During his lifetime he only published two volumes of poetry: *A Shropshire Lad* and *Poems*.

JULIA WARD HOWE (1819–1910) was a versatile writer and activist who wrote "The Battle-Hymn of the Republic," which became a popular Union song when it was published in the *Atlantic Monthly* in 1862. She was born in New York City to a banker father and a poet mother. A writer from age 16, Howe was active in the anti-slavery and women's suffrage movements.

Although she wrote or translated over 100 books in collaboration with her husband William, including works of fiction and history, the Englishwoman MARY HOWITT (1799–1888) is remembered today for a single poem so familiar it comes as a surprise to learn that anyone wrote it: her rhyming, cautionary fable for children, "The Spider and the Fly."

LANGSTON HUGHES (1902–1967) is the poet laureate of African-American experience — a popular writer of the Harlem Renaissance who gave hopeful expression to the aspirations of the oppressed, even as he decried racism and injustice. In addition to poetry, he published fiction, drama, autobiography, and translations. His work continues to serve as a model of wide empathy and social commitment.

Born in Jacksonville, Florida, JAMES WELDON JOHNSON (1871–1938) was the first African-American lawyer accepted to the Florida bar and was among the first African-American professors at New York University. A noted writer, editor, statesman, and civil rights activist during the Harlem Renaissance, he wrote the lyrics to the famous anthem "Lift Ev'ry Voice and Sing." His most ambitious work is *God's Trombones*, which he wrote while serving as Executive Secretary of the NAACP.

BEN JONSON'S (1572–1637) "Song to Celia" is known to millions as "Drink to Me Only With Thine Eyes." Jonson was educated at the prestigious Westminster School in London. He took up acting, and by

1597 he was writing original plays. Jonson's first widely acclaimed play, *Every Man in His Humour*, included William Shakespeare in its cast.

JOHN KEATS (1795 – 1821) was born in London, where he was raised by a merchant after both his parents died when he was a teenager. Before Keats's tragically early death at age 25, he was already celebrated as one of the prominent Romantic poets. He produced some of the most memorable poems of his time, including "Ode on a Grecian Urn" and the epic "Hyperion."

Journalist and poet JOYCE KILMER (1886 – 1918) was born in New Brunswick, New Jersey. Known for poetry that celebrated the common beauty of the natural world as well as his religious faith, he was killed in World War I. Kilmer was awarded by the French the prestigious Croix de Guerre (War Cross) for his bravery.

YUSEF KOMUNYAKAA's (b. 1947) poems are rooted in his experiences as an African American growing up in rural Louisiana and his service in the Vietnam War. Influenced by the jazz music he loves as well as by people's everyday speech, his poetry has won a number of awards, including the Pulitzer Prize in 1994.

EMMA LAZARUS (1849 – 1887) was born in New York City to a wealthy family and educated by private tutors. She began writing poetry as a teenager and took up the cause — through both poetry and prose — against the persecution of Jews in Russia during the 1880s. Her sonnet "The New Colossus" was engraved on the pedestal of the Statue of Liberty in 1886, memorializing the famous lines, "Give me your tired, your poor, / Your huddled masses...."

EDWARD LEAR's (1812 – 1888) father was thrown into debtor's prison when the poet was 13. One of 21 children, Lear was forced to support himself by selling his artwork. During his lifetime, he was best known for his landscape paintings, but today he is more remembered for his humorous poems such as "The Owl and the Pussy-Cat." Lear also popularized the limerick in *A Book of Nonsense*.

The son of a personal physician of Mao Zedong, LI-YOUNG LEE (b. 1957) was born in Jakarta, Indonesia, to Chinese parents. After fleeing the country, the family settled in the United States in 1964. Lee's poems have received many honors. His memoir, *The Winged Seed: A Remembrance*, won the American Book Award. The poet lives in Chicago, Illinois.

Born in Malacca, Malaysia, SHIRLEY GEOK-LIN LIM (b. 1944) was raised by her Chinese father and attended missionary schools. Although her first languages were Malay and the Hokkin dialect of Chinese, she was able to read English by the time she was six. Lim emigrated to the United States after college, settling eventually in California. Her several books of poetry include *Monsoon History: Selected Poems* and *What the Fortune Teller Didn't Say*.

Nearly forgotten today, VACHEL LINDSAY (1879–1931) briefly enjoyed international acclaim. In 1920 the English *Observer* declared him "easily the most important living American poet." He owed this fame to one of the most spellbinding recitation styles ever witnessed, and to poems like "General William Booth Enters into Heaven" and "The Congo," which seem custom made for dramatic delivery. Lindsay was also one of the first movie critics.

Born in Portland, Maine, HENRY WADSWORTH LONGFELLOW (1807–1882) displayed an interest in linguistics at an early age, eventually teaching modern languages at Harvard. His idealistic poetry struck a chord with a young country sharply divided over slavery. Poems such as the narrative *Evangeline* and "Paul Revere's Ride" made Longfellow the most popular 19th-century American poet.

Like the other Cavalier poets of 17th-century England, RICHARD LOVELACE (1618–1657) lived a legendary life as a soldier, lover, and courtier. Persecuted for his unflagging support of King Charles I, he died in dire poverty — but not before writing two of the age's most melodic and moving lyrics: "To Althea, from Prison" and "To Lucasta, Going to the Wars."

CHRISTOPHER MARLOWE (1564–1593), the son of a shoemaker, was educated at Cambridge before he joined the Lord Admiral's Theatre Company in London. Like Shakespeare, a contemporary whom he influenced, Marlowe worked as an actor as well as a dramatist. He wrote beautiful love poems and heroic plays, including *Dr. Faustus* and *The Jew of Malta*. His brilliant career, though, was cut tragically short when he was killed in a tavern fight at 29.

Today ANDREW MARVELL (1621–1678) is best known for his *carpe diem* poem "To His Coy Mistress." His wit and humor make this English metaphysical poet's work memorable. Marvell was also a talented statesman and worked as an assistant to John Milton when Milton was Oliver Cromwell's Latin secretary for foreign affairs.

Originally from Bellingham, Washington, DAVID MASON (b. 1954) currently lives outside Colorado Springs where he teaches at his alma mater, Colorado College. Mason's love for travel — he has lived in Greece and hitchhiked the British Isles — along with such tragedies as his brother's death, are major themes in his work. Also a deft essayist and critic, Mason's poetry has been collected in *The Country I Remember* and *Arrivals*.

The 1915 publication of *Spoon River Anthology* made EDGAR LEE MASTERS (1868 – 1950) famous by bringing into American poetry a scandalous subject matter and an innovative method: the secret lives and loves of a small town's citizens, told in their own voices from beyond the grave. The book was a popular and critical triumph; nothing Masters published subsequently equaled its success.

After emigrating to America from Jamaica, CLAUDE MCKAY (1890 – 1948) became a central figure of the Harlem Renaissance. Whether protesting racial and economic inequities or expressing romantic attachment, his poetry communicates its themes through vivid imagery and moving language.

Although chiefly known for his magisterial novel *Moby-Dick* and for other prose works, HERMAN MELVILLE (1819 – 1891) was also a fascinating poet who turned to the art after his serious fiction failed to find appreciative readers. His eccentric verse displays the complexity of thought and verbal richness of his novels, which has led some critics to rank him just below Walt Whitman and Emily Dickinson among 19th-century American poets.

Born in Rockland, Maine, EDNA ST. VINCENT MILLAY (1892 – 1950) as a teenager entered a national poetry contest sponsored by *The Lyric Year* magazine; her poem "Renascence" won fourth place and led to a scholarship at Vassar College. Millay was as famous during her lifetime for her red-haired beauty, unconventional lifestyle, and outspoken politics as for her poetry. Yet her passionate, formal lyrics are cherished by many readers today, fifty years after her death.

JOHN MILTON (1608 – 1674), born in London, spent six years after graduating from Cambridge at his father's country home reading the classics and writing poetry. Ardent about morals and politics, he wrote progressive tracts on divorce and freedom of the press, as well as pamphlets in support of Oliver Cromwell during England's Civil

War. Milton wrote *Paradise Lost*, one of the greatest epic poems in English, after he had gone completely blind.

The 1968 publication of his first novel *House Made of Dawn* brought N. SCOTT MOMADAY (b. 1934) a Pulitzer Prize and wide renown as the leading figure in a Native-American literary renaissance. His subsequent works in prose and poetry have shown what richness and power can result from blending Native-American oral traditions with classical European forms.

Considered "a poet's poet" for the subtlety of her thought and glittering verse technique, MARIANNE MOORE (1887–1972) was also a fascinating character who in later life became a literary celebrity — she was recognized for her cape, three-cornered hat, and baseball fanaticism as for anything she wrote. Wide renown did not come until 1951, when Moore's *Collected Poems* won the National Book and Bollingen Awards and the Pulitzer Prize.

Born in Cleveland, Ohio, MARILYN NELSON (b. 1946) is an accomplished poet, children's verse author, and translator. Her six books of poetry include *Magnificat*, *The Fields of Praise*, and *Carver: A Life in Poems*. Nelson is a Professor of English at the University of Connecticut, and is the Poet Laureate of the State of Connecticut.

YONE NOGUCHI (1875 – 1947) was the first Japanese-born writer to publish poetry in English; *The Pilgrimage* contained six haiku, a spare and direct form that inspired Ezra Pound and the Imagist movement. The poet was also the father of Isamu Noguchi, the internationally renowned sculptor and designer.

WILFRED OWEN (1893 – 1918) spent much of his short, adult life as a volunteer soldier for the British military during World War I. He wrote vivid and terrifying poems about modern warfare. Owen was killed by machinegun fire just days before the end of the war.

DOROTHY PARKER's (1893–1967) biting wit made her a legend, but it also masked her lonely struggle with depression. A member of the Algonquin Round Table group of writers, she wrote criticism for *Vogue*, *Vanity Fair*, and later the *New Yorker*. During the 1930s Parker moved to Hollywood, where she worked on such films as *A Star Is Born*, for which she won an Academy Award.

One of the first women to acquire fame as a writer in England, KATHERINE PHILIPS (1631 – 1664) addressed poems of love and companionship to the women in her circle, called "Society of Friendship." She was known as "The Matchless Orinda" for the pseudonym she adopted within the group and as "the English Sappho" for her similarities to the ancient Greek poetess of Lesbos.

EDGAR ALLAN POE (1809–1849) was born in Boston, Massachusetts, and raised in Richmond, Virginia, by a foster family. In his poetry and fiction, Poe explored the dark inner workings of the mind. He is credited with being a forerunner of horror fiction and of the short story as a literary form. After years of depression and alcoholism, Poe died mysteriously at age 40.

ALEXANDER POPE (1688–1744) was born in London to a Roman Catholic family. A childhood sickness left him with stunted height, a curved spine, and ill health for the rest of his life. Pope earned fame and great financial success as a poet, satirist, and translator. He is perhaps best remembered for his mastery of the heroic couplet, as in *An Essay on Man* and "The Rape of the Lock."

EZRA POUND (1885–1972) was born in Hailey, Idaho, grew up near Philadelphia, but lived much of his adult life overseas. In his early career he was the influential and controversial leader of Imagism and Vorticism. He also championed young writers, including H.D., T.S. Eliot, and Robert Frost. Among his best-known works are "In a Station of the Metro," "Hugh Selwyn Mauberley," and *The Cantos*, a ranging, lifelong work that expounded his political and economic theories.

Before his execution for treason, SIR WALTER RALEGH (1552–1618) won fame as an explorer of the New World — both for voyages to Roanoke Island in present-day North Carolina (whose capital is named after him), and to Venezuela in search of El Dorado, the mythical city of gold. Also a scholar and a gifted lyric poet, Ralegh brought glory to Elizabethan England along with the potatoes and tobacco he is said to have introduced there.

DUDLEY RANDALL (1914–2000) published his first poem in the *Detroit Free Press* when he was thirteen. After earning degrees in English and library science, Randall worked as a librarian until his 1974 retirement. He established Broadside Press in 1965, which became an important publisher of African-American poets and political writers. Randall translated Russian writers, and experimented with a variety of styles in his own poetry.

EDWIN ARLINGTON ROBINSON (1869 – 1935) is America's poet laureate of unhappiness. In patiently crafted verse of great sonority, he portrays men and women suffering from life's ordeals yet striving to understand and master their fates. Robinson's tragic vision had its roots in a youth spent in the small town of Gardiner, Maine. So sensitive he claimed he came into the world "with his skin inside out," he once told a fellow poet that at six he had sat in a rocking chair and wondered why he'd been born.

CHRISTINA ROSSETTI (1830 – 1894) was born in London to an artistic family — her brother was the famous poet and painter Dante Gabriel Rossetti and her house was a regular meeting place for the group of artists later called the Pre-Raphaelite Brotherhood. As a devout Anglican, Rossetti called off a two-year engagement when her fiancé converted to Roman Catholicism. Despite a lifetime of illness, Rossetti continued to write poetry. Today she is best known for her collection *Goblin Market and Other Poems*.

Poet, novelist, essayist, and children's book author, BENJAMIN ALIRE SÁENZ (b. 1954) grew up on a cotton farm in New Mexico speaking only Spanish until he started elementary school. Although his education eventually took him to Denver, Belguim, Iowa, and California, Sáenz settled in the border region between Texas and New Mexico — an area that remains central to his writing.

Though first made famous for the urban aesthetic of his poems about the people and city of Chicago, CARL SANDBURG (1878 – 1967) was born with humble working class roots in Galesburg, Illinois. An activist, poet, and author, he won two Pulitzer Prizes, the first in 1940 for his biography of Abraham Lincoln and the second in 1951 for his *Collected Poems*.

Actor, dramatist, and poet, WILLIAM SHAKESPEARE (1564 – 1616) is the most highly regarded writer in the English language. Born in Stratford-Upon-Avon in England, Shakespeare wrote 38 plays, including *Othello*, *A Midsummer Night's Dream*, *Hamlet*, and *Romeo and Juliet*. His epic narrative poems and 154 sonnets include some of the world's most quoted lines.

Born into a wealthy family in Sussex, England, PERCY BYSSHE SHELLEY (1792 – 1822) was expelled from Oxford for writing *The Necessity of Atheism*. His radical lifestyle at times detracted from the appreciation of his work. He called poets "the unacknowledged legislators of the world." In Shelley's short life—he drowned while sailing at age 29—he produced gorgeous lyrical poetry quintessential of the Romantic Era. He is perhaps best remembered for the mythical poem *Prometheus Unbound* and for *Adonais*, an elegy to his friend John Keats.

CHARLOTTE SMITH (1749–1806) wrote *Elegiac Sonnets* in 1783 while she was in debtor's prison with her husband and children. William Wordsworth identified her as an important influence on the Romantic movement. She published several longer works that celebrated the individual while deploring social injustice and the British class system.

Born in Reading, Pennsylvania, WALLACE STEVENS (1879–1955) is one of most significant American poets of the 20th century. The consummate businessman-poet, Stevens had a successful career as a corporate lawyer when his first book of poems, *Harmonium*, was published in 1923. However, he did not receive widespread recognition from the literary community until the release of his *Collected Poems* in 1954.

JONATHAN SWIFT (1667–1745) was born to English parents in Dublin, Ireland, and his family moved throughout Great Britain. Deeply involved in politics and religion, Swift became one of the first prose satirists. His masterpiece is *Gulliver's Travels*. Swift's sharp wit carried over into his poetry, as in the mock elegy for himself, "Verses on the Death of Dr. Swift."

A native of Calcutta, India, who wrote in Bengali and often translated his own work into English, RABINDRANATH TAGORE (1861–1941) won the Nobel Prize for Literature in 1913—the first Asian to receive the honor. He wrote poetry, fiction, drama, essays, and songs; promoted reforms in education, aesthetics and religion; and in his late sixties he even turned to the visual arts, producing 2,500 paintings and drawings before his death.

SARA TEASDALE (1884–1933) was born in St. Louis, Missouri. She won fame in her day as a sensitive soul whose simple, poignant poems addressed beauty and loss. Teasdale's *Love Songs* received the first Pulitzer Prize for poetry in 1918.

ALFRED, LORD TENNYSON (1809–1892) was born one of 12 children to a wealthy family in Lincolnshire, England. With poems such as *In Memoriam*, an elegy for a friend, and *Idylls of the King*, a long narrative, Tennyson became the most popular English poet of his time. Queen Victoria made him Poet Laureate in 1850. He is buried in Westminster Abbey.

DYLAN THOMAS (1914 – 1953) grew up in Wales, however, he lived much of his life in London. At age 20, he published *Eighteen Poems* to instant acclaim. Thomas gave four reading tours of the United States, earning renown for mesmerizing performances and a boisterous personality. His last drinking binge at the White Horse Tavern in New York City led to his death at age 39.

An important writer of the Harlem Renaissance, JEAN TOOMER (1894 – 1967) was born in Washington, DC, and was the grandson of the first governor of African-American descent in the United States. A poet, playwright, and novelist, Toomer's most famous work, *Cane*, was published in 1923 and was hailed by critics for its literary experimentation and portrayal of African-American characters and culture.

AMY UYEMATSU (b. 1947) grew up in southern California. Her poetry grows out of the conflict between her wish to belong to the culture around her and her strong sense of ethnic identity — like many Japanese Americans during World War II, her parents and grandparents were interned. A high school math teacher, she has published three collections: *30 Miles from J-Town*; *Nights of Fire, Nights of Rain*; and *Stone Bow Prayer*.

Elected to Parliament at age 16, EDMUND WALLER (1606 – 1687) quickly gained a reputation as a masterful orator. He was also a celebrated lyric poet long before the publication of his *Poems* in 1645. Despite his eloquent efforts to placate both Oliver Cromwell and Charles II, Waller was forced into exile for nearly a decade. His highly refined work, particularly his heroic couplets, were much admired by Alexander Pope and John Dryden.

Born in the Senegal-Gambia region of West Africa, PHILLIS WHEATLEY (ca. 1753 – 1784) arrived in Boston on a slave ship in 1761. When Mrs. Susanna Wheatley purchased her as a personal servant she named Phillis after the ship. After 16 months Wheatley could read and understand any part of the Bible, and she began writing poetry at age 12. Her poem "To the Right Honorable William, Earl of Dartmouth" compares her enslaved state with that of the colonies under Britain's rule, denouncing both.

WALT WHITMAN (1819 – 1892) is America's world poet — a latter-day successor to Homer, Virgil, Dante, and Shakespeare. In his *Leaves of Grass*, first published in 1855 and revised and expanded for the rest of his life, he celebrated democracy, nature, love, and friendship. This monumental work chanted praises to the body as well as to the soul, and found beauty and reassurance even in death.

The 1866 publication of his long poem *Snow-Bound* brought JOHN GREENLEAF WHITTIER (1807 – 1892) popular acclaim and financial security. But literary success was of secondary importance to him: his priorities were dictated by his Quaker faith and his courageous battle against slavery. Whittier was born and raised on a farm near Haverhill, Massachusetts, and felt a strong kinship throughout his life with the hard-working, rural poor.

Born in Rutherford, WILLIAM CARLOS WILLIAMS (1883 – 1963) spent almost his entire life in his native New Jersey. He was a medical doctor, poet, novelist, essayist, and playwright. With Ezra Pound and H.D., Williams was a leading poet of the Imagist movement and often wrote of American subjects and themes. Though his career was initially overshadowed by other poets, Williams became an inspiration to the Beat generation in the 1950s and 60s.

WILLIAM WORDSWORTH (1770 – 1850), born in Cumbria, England, began writing poetry in grammar school. Before graduating from college, he went on a walking tour of Europe, which deepened his love for nature and his sympathy for the common man, both major themes in his poetry. Wordsworth is best known for *Lyrical Ballads*, co-written with Samuel Taylor Coleridge, and *The Prelude*, a Romantic epic on the "growth of a poet's mind."

Born in Kent, England, SIR THOMAS WYATT (1503 – 1542) was an ambassador to France and Italy for King Henry VIII. Wyatt's travels abroad exposed him to different forms of poetry, which he adapted for the English language — most notably, the sonnet. Rumored to be Anne Boleyn's lover, he spent a month in the Tower of London until Boleyn's execution for adultery. Many consider his poem "Whoso List to Hunt" to be about Boleyn.

Like her friend Edna St. Vincent Millay, ELINOR WYLIE (1885 – 1928) was as famous during the 1920s for her exotic beauty and tempestuous love life as for her writing. Born in Somerville, New Jersey, she spent time in England, then returned to New York, where she published her first important book of poems, *Nets to Catch the Wind*. Before her untimely death at 43, she published four books of poems and four novels — all notable for their energy, cleverness, and formal polish.

Born in Dublin, Ireland, WILLIAM BUTLER YEATS (1865 – 1939) was an enormously influential poet and playwright, whose work formed a clear link between the Romantic and Modern eras. His strong nationalism appeared in his poetry through the recurrent themes of Irish mythology and folklore. Yeats became deeply involved in Irish politics and was even appointed a senator of the Irish Free State. In 1923 he was awarded the Nobel Prize for Literature.

CREDITS

ACKNOWLEDGMENTS

Many people helped produce the *Poetry Out Loud Anthology*. Sean Francis, Kimberly Gooden, James McNeel, Jon Mooallem, and Amanda Sumner wrote biographies of the poets for both the print and on-line editions. Bill Drenttel, Geoff Halber, and Don Whelan of Winterhouse Studio designed and typeset the book. Fred Courtright secured permissions for poems under copyright. Dillon Tracy helped manage the production schedules. Erika Koss, Garrick Davis, Pamela Kirkpatrick, and Elizabeth Stigler proofread the manuscript under tight deadlines. Finally, thanks are due to Ian Lancashire and the many other editors who have contributed to the University of Toronto's *Representative Poetry On-Line*. Their efforts aided indirectly in producing this physical anthology and directly in creating its companion web-based anthology.